ONDORI

EMBROIDERY AND CROSS
FOR FRAMING

★Published by Ondorisha Publishers, Ltd.,
  32 Nishigoken-cho, Shinjuku-ku, Tokyo 162, Japan.
★Sole Overseas Distributors: Japan Publications Trading Co., Ltd.,
  P. O. Box 5030 Tokyo International, Tokyo, Japan.
★Distributed in the United States by Kodansha International/USA, Ltd.
  through Harper & Row, Publishers, Inc., 10 East 53rd Street, New York, New York 10022.

10 9 8 7 6 5 4 3 2

★ISBN 0-87040-537-3
  Printed in Japan.

FLOWERS

FRAME   36 cm by 31.5 cm
Instructions on page 41.

1

FRAME   19 cm square
Instructions on page 42.

PANEL 23 cm by 21 cm
Instructions on page 44.

PANEL   23 cm by 21 cm
Instructions on page 45.

4

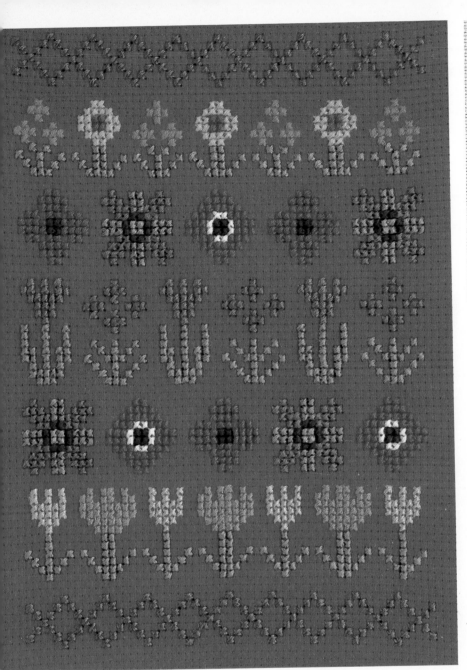

PANELS 18 cm by 13.5 cm
Instructions on page 46.

5

DOOR HANGING 49 cm by 9.5 cm
Instructions on page 47.

FRAME 32 cm by 26 cm
Instructions on page 48.

FRAMES 27 cm by 22 cm
Instructions on page 49.

FRAME 19.5 cm square
Instructions on page 51.

FRAME 32 cm by 26 cm
Instructions on page 51.

LANDSCAPES

PANEL 38.5 cm by 23.5 cm
Instructions on page 74.

FRAME   17 cm square
Instructions on page 53.

FRAME   19 cm square
Instructions on page 54.

FRAMES 37 cm by 44.5 cm
Instructions on page 85.

18

FRAMES 18 cm squar
Instructions on page 5.

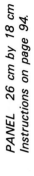

PANEL 26 cm by 18 cm
Instructions on page 94.

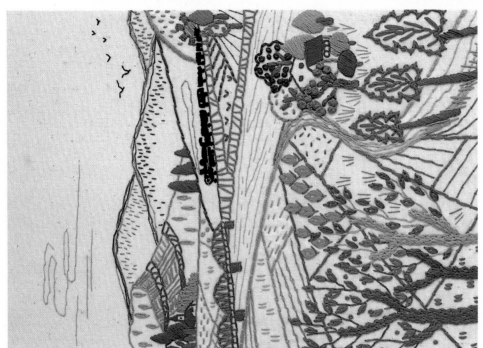

PANEL 26 cm by 18 cm
Instructions on page 97.

FRAME 26 cm by 32 cm
Instructions on page 84.

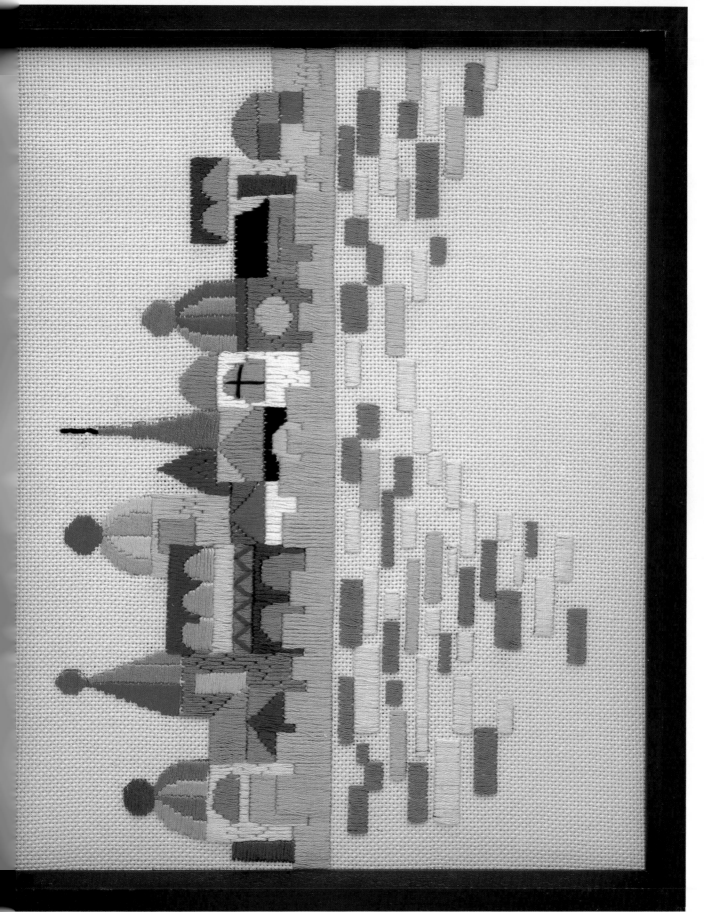

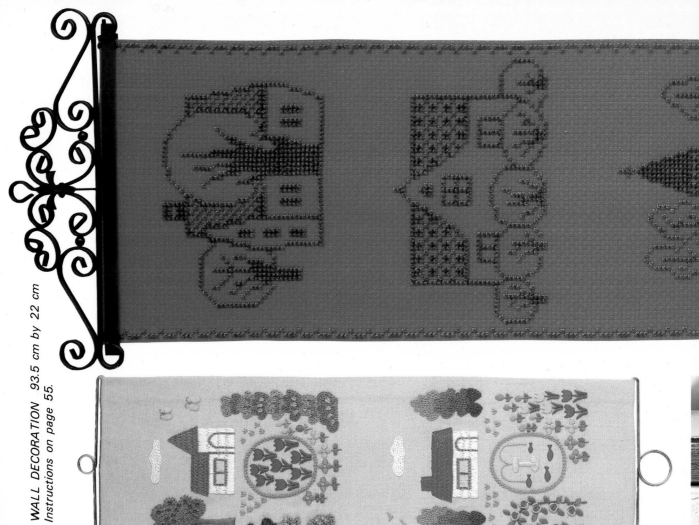

WALL DECORATION 93.5 cm by 22 cm
Instructions on page 55.

WALL DECORATION 50.5 cm by 15 cm
Instructions on page 62.

TAPESTRY 24.5 cm by 32 cm
Instructions on page 82.

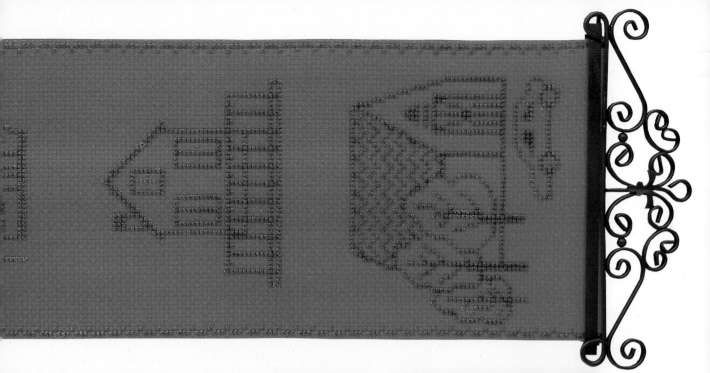

24

FRAMES 13 cm square
Instructions on page 60.

FAIRY TALES

FRAMES   19.5 cm square
Instructions on page 64.

25

FRAME 23 cm square
Instructions on page 77.

26

FRAME 19 cm square
Instructions on page 90.

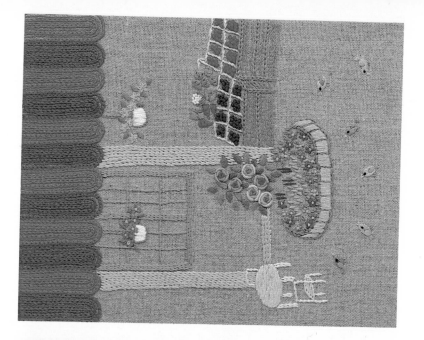

PANELS 23 cm by 18 cm
Instructions on page 91.

TAPESTRY 34.5 cm by 49 cm
Instructions on page 87.

28

30

FRAMES 44 cm by 41 cm
Instructions on page 78.

PANEL 30 cm by 20 cm
Instructions on page 65.

31

WALL DECORATION 30 cm by 15 cm
Instructions on page 66.

WALL DECORATION 70.5 cm by 20 cm
Instructions on page 70.

WALL DECORATION 43 cm by 20 cm
Instructions on page 67.

34

FRAMES
37 cm by 33 cm
Instructions on page 68.

FRAME 43.5 cm by 36 cm
Instructions on page 72.

35

GEOMETRIC DESIGNS

40

PANELS 15 cm square
Instructions on page 99.

Instructions

FLOWER BASKET Shown on page 1

Fabric: White Java
canvas, 35 mesh to
... cm; 39 cm by 34
...

Thread: D.M.C
...strand embroidery
...ss:

...2 skeins each of
...ornflower Blue
...93), Brilliant Green
...03); 1 skein each
... Cerise (604),
...um (554), Rasp-
...rry Red (3689),
...illiant Green
...01), and Myrtle
...ay (924); ½ skein
...h of Cerise (601),
...olet Mauve (327),
...aspberry Red
...688), Yellow
...een (734) and
...nary Yellow
...72); small amount
...h of Soft Pink
...76), Cornflower
...ue (792) and
...nary Yellow
...1).

...me: White, 32.5
... by 28 cm (inside
...asurements).

...ished size: Same
... as frame.

...ge: One square
... design equals one
...are mesh of fab-
...

...ections: Match
...ters of fabric and
...ign. Cross-stitch
...indicated. Mount
... frame.

*Use 6-strand floss.

△ = 554	✚ = 3689	⊡ = 776	▲ = 792	▨ = 793	■ = 924	◎ = 3688	⊠ = 327	V = 703
▨ = 701	⊕ = 734	◻ = 604	⦿ = 601	⊠ = 972	⊠ = 971			

WILD FLOWERS

Shown on page 2, top

Fabric: Olive-green Irish linen, 21 cm square.
Thread: D.M.C 6-strand embroidery floss:
Small amount each of Moss Green (966), Brilliant Green (702), Fire Red (900), Canary Yellow (972), Parma Violet (208), Raspberry Red (3689) and White.

Frame: White, 15 cm square (inside measurements).
Finished size: Same size as frame.
Directions: Match centers of fabric and design, and transfe[r]
design to fabric. Embroider. Mount and frame.

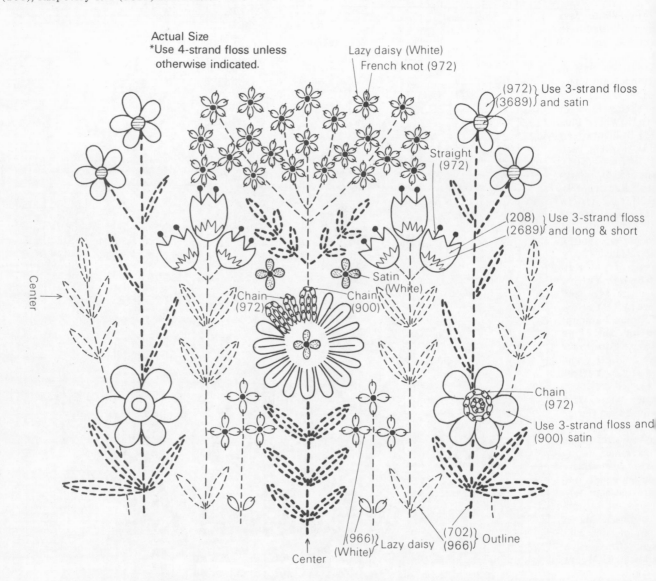

Actual Size
*Use 4-strand floss unless otherwise indicated.

Lazy daisy (White)
French knot (972)

(972)⎫ Use 3-strand floss
(3689)⎭ and satin

Straight (972)

(208)⎫ Use 3-strand floss
(2689)⎭ and long & short

Satin (White)

Chain (972)   Chain (972)   Chain (900)

Center

Chain (972)

Use 3-strand floss and (900) satin

Center

(966)⎫ Lazy daisy
(White)⎭

(702)⎫ Outline
(966)⎭

RED ROSES   Shown on page 2, bottom & page 3

Fabric: White Irish linen, 36 cm by 29 cm.
Thread: D.M.C 6-strand embroidery floss:
Right frame
½ skein each of Tangerine Yellow (740, 741) and Red Brown (921); small amount each of Episcopal Purple (718), Raspberry Red (3688, 3689), Mahogany (400, 301, 402), Old Rose (3354), Magenta Rose (961), Fire Red (900, 947), Geranium Red (754), Moss Green (469, 471,472), Scarab Green (3347), Saffron (725, 726), Buttercup Yellow (444), Tangerine Yellow (742), Copper Green (831, 832) and Umber (433, 435, 436).

Left frame
3 skeins of Poppy (666).
Frame: 29.5 cm by 23 cm.
Finished size: Same size as frame.
Directions: Match centers of fabric and design, and trans[fer]
design to fabric. Embroider. Mount and frame.

ble lazy daisy (3347)
French knot (444) (3689) (3699) (3689)
Outline (402)
Outline (402)
D
A
C
B
Outline filling (469)
Actual Size
(472)
(402)
Outline (400)
(400)
(469)
Outline (469)
Fly (469)
(740)
(741)
French knot Outline (742)
French knot (832)
(444)
(961)
(301)
(3699)
(718)
(3354)
Chain (435)
(3347)
(436)
(472)
(725)
(726)
Long & short
E
D
F
E
C
C
D
E
472)
D
E
C
D
C
F
D
E
E
(831)
(832)
Outline filling
(469)
(3347)
Outline
(3347)
C
F
A
B
D
F
D
C
A
B
(718)
(471)
Long & short (471)
(3347)
Lazy daisy (3688)
Long & short
(472)
Double lazy daisy (3347)
(3688)
Lazy daisy (718)
(3689)
(718)
(718)
(718)
(3347)
(718)
ble lazy (47)
(718)
(3689)
(3347) { Outline Variation of Lazy daisy (Refer to p. 71)
Use 4-strand floss and Outline { (436) (433) (435)
.. 900
.. 947
.. 740
.. 741
.. 921
.. 754
Use 3-strand floss.
Outline (831)
Center
Long & short (471)

Use 3-strand floss and satin stitch unless otherwise indicated.

Roses: { = 4-strand floss, closed buttonhole stitch
= 3-strand floss, long-and-short stitch

Wrap thread around needle twice for French knot unless otherwise indicated. Use 4-strand floss to outline roses for picture on p. 2 using outline stitch. Refer to photograph for outlining leaves and vase.

43

GIRL WITH FLOWER BASKET   Shown on page 4, top

Fabric: White plain weave linen, 33 cm by 31 cm.
Thread: D.M.C 6-strand embroidery floss:
½ skein of Soft Pink (776); small amount each of Soft Pink (818, 819), Geranium Pink (891), Magenta Rose (961), Geranium Red (351, 353), Turkey Red (321), Greenish Gray (598), Pistachio Green (320), Laurel Green (988), Tangerine Yellow (743), Umber (436), Flame Red (606), Coffee Brown (938), Cerise (600), Umber Gold (977), Smoke Gray (640) and Black (310).

Finished size: 23 cm by 21 cm (size of display panel).
Directions: Match centers of fabric and design, and transfer design to fabric. Embroider. Mount onto display panel.

Actual Size
*Use 3-strand floss unless
otherwise indicated.

Back (776)

(776)
(818)
(819)

Lazy daisy (743)

Satin (436)

(598)
(743)   Satin

Outline (938)

Random cross and 2-strand floss

Satin (988)

Outline Satin   (320)

Straight and 2-strand floss (310)

(310) Back 2-strand floss   Satin

Satin (776)

Fly (606)

Satin (353)

Long & short (606)

Straight Satin   (938)

Center

Satin (977)

Outline (310)

Closed buttonhole (818)

(640)

Satin (640)

(321)
(351)   Long & short

Fill in with back stitch

Fill in with random cross-stitch using 2-strand floss. (818) before outlining with outline stitch.

Outline (961)

Random cross and 2-strand floss

Outline (600)

Satin (891)

Straight Outline   (938)

Center

44

DANCING BUTTERFLIES   Shown on page 4, bottom

Fabric: White plain weave linen, 33 cm by 31 cm.
Thread: D.M.C 6-strand embroidery floss:
Small amount each of Moss Green (471), Pistachio Green
(320), Greenish Gray (598), Umber (435, 436), Coffee
Brown (938), Garnet Red (309), Soft Pink (776, 818),
Geranium Red (948), Peony Rose (956), Tangerine Yellow
(741, 743), Canary Yellow (972), Sky Blue (517), Azure
Blue (3325) and Black (310).

Finished size: 23 cm by 21 cm (size of display panel).
Directions: Match centers of fabric and design, and transfer
design to fabric. Embroider. Mount onto display panel.

Actual Size   *Use 3-strand floss and outline stitch
unless otherwise indicated.

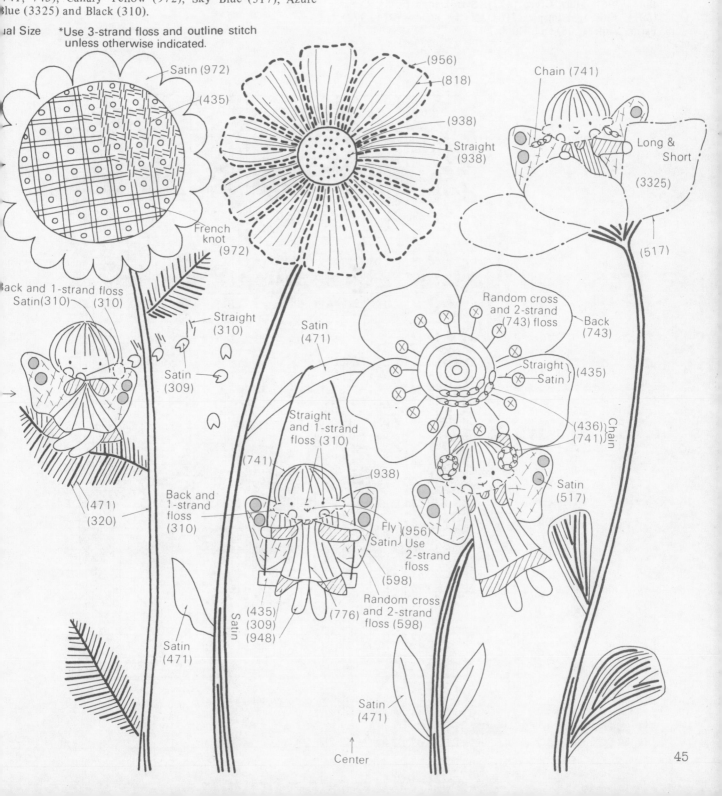

FLOWER GARDEN

Shown on page 5

Fabric: Indian cloth, 52 mesh to 10 cm; 28 cm by 24 cm.
Two pieces: red and white.
Thread: D.M.C 6-strand embroidery floss:
Small amount each of Beige (3022), Brilliant Green (703), Peony Rose (957), Soft Pink (899), Sky Blue (518), Royal Blue (796), Moss Green (472), Sevres Blue (798), Cerise (601), Episcopal Purple (718), Canary Yellow (971, 972), Parma Violet (208) and White.

Finished size: 18 cm by 14 cm (size of display panel).
Gauge: One square of design equals one square mesh of fabric.
Directions: Match centers of fabric and design. Cross-stitch as indicated using four strands of floss. Mount onto display panel.

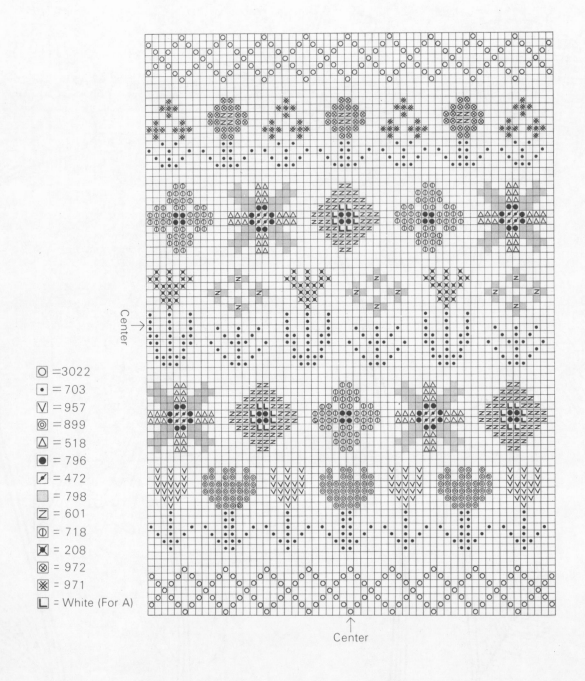

O = 3022
• = 703
V = 957
◎ = 899
△ = 518
● = 796
◪ = 472
▨ = 798
Z = 601
Φ = 718
⊠ = 208
⊗ = 972
⊛ = 971
L = White (For A)

Center

Center

DOOR HANGING   Shown on page 8

Fabric: Dark brown Java canvas, 35 mesh to 10 cm; 40 cm by 30 cm.
Thread: D.M.C 6-strand embroidery floss:
1 skein of Episcopal Purple (718); ½ skein each of Geranium Pink (891), Emerald Green (910); small amount each of Dark Brown (3033), Yellow Green (734) and Plum (552).
Ring: Reg ring, 3.8 cm inner diameter.
Finished size: 47 cm long.
Gauge: One square of design equals one square mesh of fabric.
Directions: Cross-stitch as indicated using six strands of floss.
Finish as shown in Finishing Diagram.

Loop
(make 1)

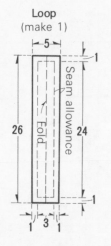

Finishing Diagram

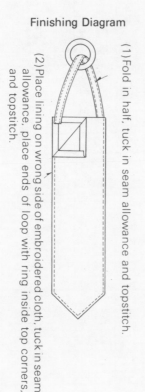

(1) Fold in half, tuck in seam allowance and topstitch.

(2) Place lining on wrong side of embroidered cloth, tuck in seam allowance, place ends of loop with ring inside top corners, and topstitch.

● = 910
Ⅴ = 891
Ⓞ = 3033
Ⅹ = 734
△ = 718
⊥ = 552

47

ROSES IN BLUE VASE   Shown on page 9

Fabric: Beige congress canvas, 70 mesh to 10 cm; 36 cm by 30 cm.

Thread: D.M.C 6-strand embroidery floss:

I skein each of Garnet Red (335), Old Rose (3354), Soft Pink (3326), and Forget-me-not Blue (825); ½ skein each of Old Rose (3350), Garnet Red (309), Soft Pink (899), Faded Pink (221, 223), Parakeet Green (904), Scarab Green (3347), Indigo (311), Umber (433); small amount each of Scarlet (814, 815), Moss Green (935, 937, 469), Pistachio Green (319) and Forget-me-not Blue (828).

Frame: 30 cm by 24 cm (inside measurements).

Finished size: Same size as frame.

Gauge: One square of design equals two-square mesh o fabric.

Directions: Match centers of fabric and design. Cross-stitch a indicated using four strands of floss. Mount and frame.

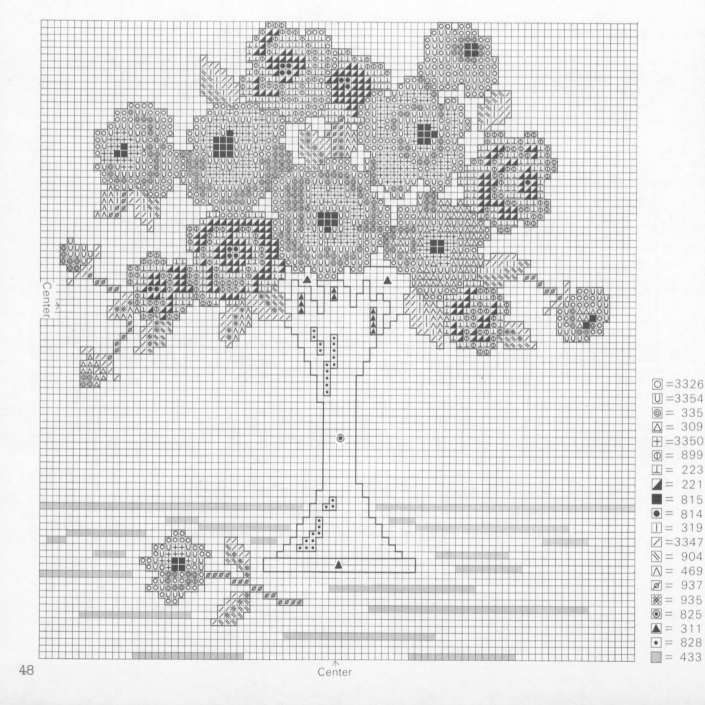

⊙	=3326
⋃	=3354
◎	= 335
△	= 309
⊞	=3350
⏀	= 899
⊥	= 223
◪	= 221
■	= 815
●	= 814
‖	= 319
⁄	=3347
◳	= 904
∧	= 469
⬟	= 937
✖	= 935
◉	= 825
▲	= 311
•	= 828
▨	= 433

48

Center

BLUE AND ORANGE CATTLEYAS

Shown on page 10

Fabric: Off-white Irish linen, 25 cm by 20 cm.
Thread: D.M.C 6-strand embroidery floss:
Top
Small amount each of Umber (433), Fire Red (900, 947),
Green (3052), Scarlet (498), Tangerine Yellow (741) and
Golden Yellow (783).

Bottom
Small amount each of Forget-me-not Blue (824), Peacock
Blue (807), Beige (3022, 3023), Brilliant Green (702), Royal
Blue (797) and Plum (554).
Finished size: Same size as frame.
Directions: Match centers of fabric and design. Embroider.
Mount and frame.

Actual Size

*Use 1-strand floss for random cross.
 Use 2-strand floss and satin stitch unless otherwise indicated.

Threads in ( )for top picture on p. 10; those in
[ ] for bottom.

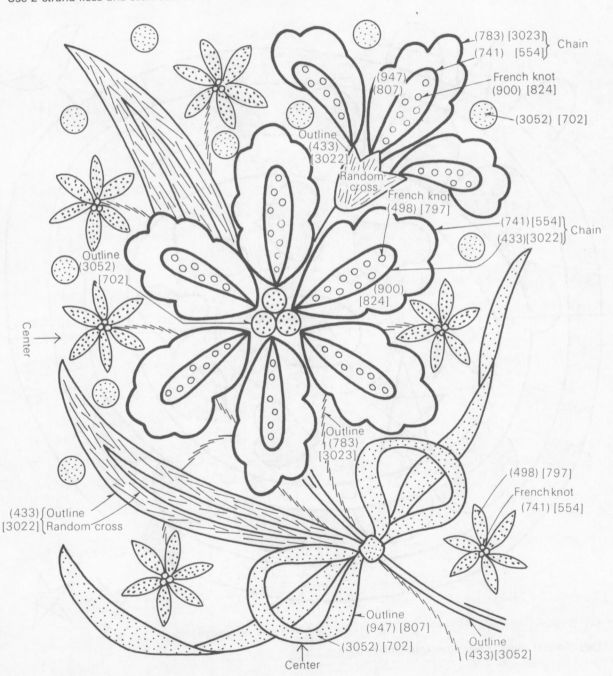

HANA SUN   Shown on page 11

Fabric: Unbleached lightweight canvas, 24 cm square.
Thread: D.M.C 6-strand embroidery floss:
1 skein each of Episcopal Purple (718), Flame Red (606), small amount each of Emerald Green (910), Canary Yellow (973), Royal Blue (820), Fire Red (947) and Black (310).

Frame: 34 cm square (inside measurements).
Finished size: 17.5 cm square (embroidered area).
Directions: Match centers of fabric and design, and transfer design to fabric. Embroider. Mount and frame.

Actual Size

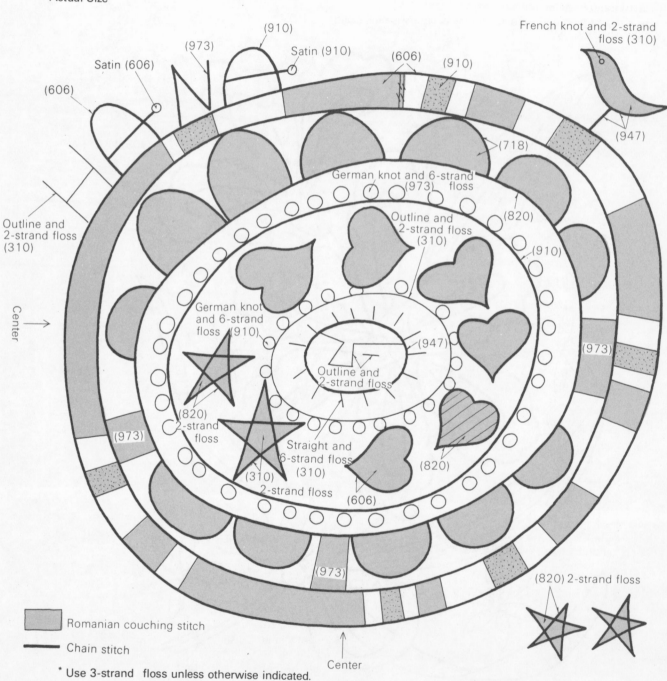

French knot and 2-strand floss (310)

(910)
(973)
Satin (910)
(606)
(910)
Satin (606)
(606)
(947)

(718)
German knot and 6-strand floss
(973)
Outline and 2-strand floss (310)

Outline and 2-strand floss (310)
(820)
(910)

German knot and 6-strand floss (910)
(947)
(910)

Center

(973)

(820)
2-strand floss

Outline and 2-strand floss

(973)
(820)

(310)
Straight and 6-strand floss
(310)
2-strand floss
(606)
(820)

(973)
(820) 2-strand floss

Romanian couching stitch

Chain stitch

Center

* Use 3-strand floss unless otherwise indicated.

50

SWEET PEAS

Shown on page 12

Fabric: Cobalt blue Irish linen, 18 cm square (cut on the bias).
Thread: D.M.C 6-strand embroidery floss:
Small amount each of Peony Rose (956), Soft Pink (818) and Brilliant Green (703).

Frame: 12 cm square (inside measurements).
Finished size: Same size as frame.
Directions: Transfer design to fabric. Embroider. Mount and frame.

Actual Size
*Use chain stitch and 3-strand floss.

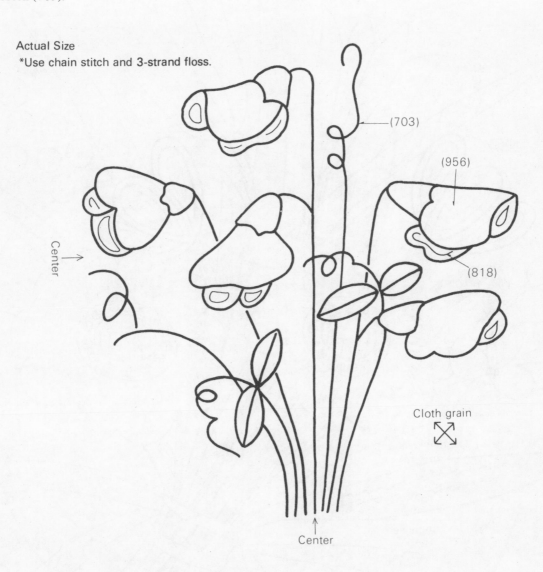

(703)

(956)

(818)

Center

Cloth grain

Center

FLOWER BOUQUET

Shown on page 13

Fabric: Cream Irish linen, 21 cm square.
Thread: D.M.C 6-strand embroidery floss:
½ skein each of Emerald Green (911), Laurel Green (988), Garnet Red (309), Tangerine Yellow (740), small amount each of Pistachio Green (367), Emerald Green (913), Scarab Green (3348), Geramium Red (892), Cerise (600), Geranium Pink (894), Peony Rose (957), Royal Blue (797), Sevres Blue (798), Plum (552, 554), Fire Red (947), Tangerine Yellow (742), Buttercup Yellow (444), Saffron (727) and Light Yellow (3078).
Frame: Green, 15 cm square (inside measurements).
Finished size: Same size as frame.
Directions: Match centers of fabric and design, and transfer design to fabric. Embroider. Mount and frame.

51

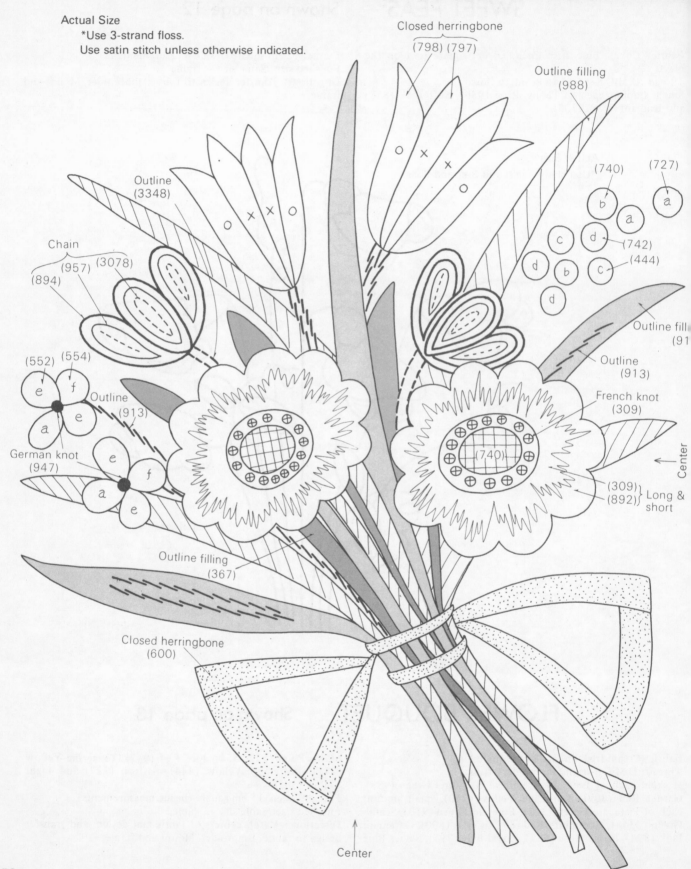

Actual Size
*Use 3-strand floss.
Use satin stitch unless otherwise indicated.

Closed herringbone
(798) (797)

Outline filling
(988)

Outline
(3348)

(740)   (727)

b   a

c   d

a

(742)

d   b   c   (444)

d

Outline fill
(91

Chain
(957) (3078)
(894)

Outline fill
(91

Outline
(913)

French knot
(309)

(552) (554)

e   f

a   e

Outline
(913)

German knot
(947)

e

a   f

e

(740)

Center

(309)
(892)

Long &
short

Outline filling
(367)

Closed herringbone
(600)

Center

52

HOUSE WITH RED ROOF   Shown on page 16, top

Fabric: Cobalt blue Irish linen, 21 cm square.
Thread: D.M.C 6-strand embroidery floss:
½ skein each of Peacock Green (991), Sage Green (3013),
small amount each of Green (3051, 3053), Laurel Green
(988), Scarab Green (3347), Brilliant Green (700, 701), Fire
Red (900), Flame Red (608), Emerald Green (912), Almond
Green (502), Drab (610), Sepia (3371), Red Brown (920),

Sevres Blue (799), White and Saffron (726).
Frame: 15 cm square (inside measurements).
Finished size: Same size as frame.
Directions: Match centers of fabric and design, and transfer
design to fabric. Embroider. Mount and frame.

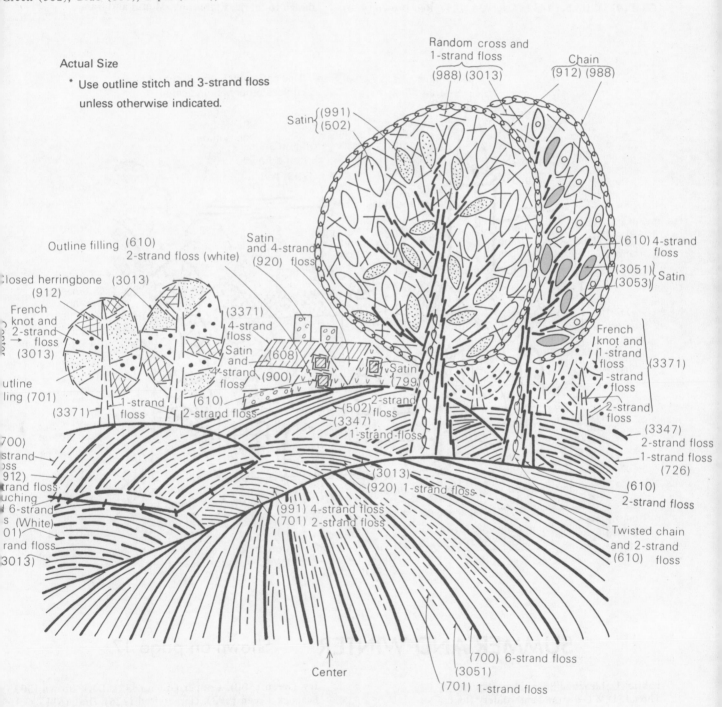

Actual Size

* Use outline stitch and 3-strand floss
  unless otherwise indicated.

Random cross and
1-strand floss
(988) (3013)

Chain
(912) (988)

Satin {(991)
{(502)

(610) 4-strand
floss

(3051) } Satin
(3053) }

French
knot and
1-strand
floss
(3371)

1-strand
floss

2-strand
floss

(3347)
2-strand floss

1-strand floss
(726)

(610)
2-strand floss

Twisted chain
and 2-strand
(610) floss

Outline filling (610)
2-strand floss (white)

Satin
and 4-strand
(920) floss

Closed herringbone (3013)
(912)

French
knot and
2-strand
floss
(3013)

(3371)
4-strand
floss

Satin
and
4-strand
floss

(608)

(900)

Satin
(799)

Outline
lling (701)
(3371)

1-strand
floss

(610)
2-strand floss

(502)
(3347)
1-strand floss

(3013)
(920) 1-strand floss

700)
strand
oss
912)
rand floss
uching
6-strand
s (White)
01)
rand floss
3013)

(991) 4-strand floss
(701) 2-strand floss

Center

(700) 6-strand floss
(3051)
(701) 1-strand floss

53

CHURCH AND TOWN

Shown on page 16, bottom

Fabric: Beige Irish linen, 21 cm square.
Thread: D.M.C 6-strand embroidery floss:
½ skein of White; small amount each of Raspberry Red (3688), Faded Pink (224, 225), Soft Pink (818), Coffee Brown (898), Pistachio Green (367, 320, 368), Green (3053), Yellow Green (730), Terra-cotta (356, 758), Beaver Gray (645), Indigo (939, 336), Peacock Green (992), Umber Gold (975), Umber (433, 436, 738, 739), Red Brown (920),

Moss Green (937), Copper Green (830), Mahogany (402), Almond Green (502, 503, 504), Cornflower Blue (793), Azure Blue (775), Cream (746), Canary Yellow (972), Drab (611, 613), Smoke Gray (640) and Beige Brown (841, 842).
Frame: Green, 15 cm square (inside measurements).
Finished size: 13 cm square (embroidered area).
Directions: Match centers of fabric and design, and transfer design to fabric. Embroider. Mount and frame.

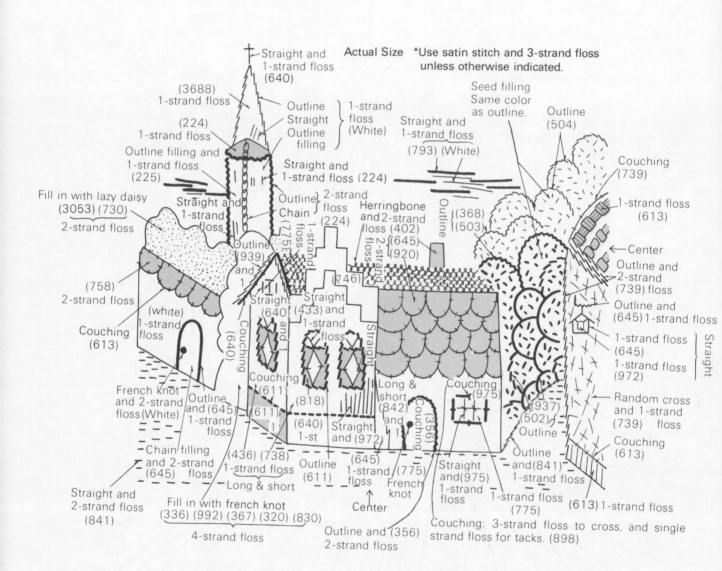

Actual Size   *Use satin stitch and 3-strand floss unless otherwise indicated.

SUMMER AND WINTER

Shown on page 17

Fabric: Unbleached linen, 21 cm square.
Thread: D.M.C 6-strand embroidery floss:
Summer
Small amount each of Pistachio Green (367, 320, 368, 369),

Ivy Green (500), Copper Green (832), Dark Brown (3033), Peacock Green (993), Garnet Red (326), Drab (611), Coffee Brown (898) and Black (310).

Winter

½ skein of Coffee Brown (898), small amount each of Copper Green (832), Dark Brown (3033), Peacock Green (993), Garnet Red (326), Drab (611) and Black (310).
Frame: Gold, 15 cm square.
Finished size: Same size as frame.
Directions: Match centers of fabric and design, and transfer design to fabric. Embroider. Mount and frame.

Actual Size *Use 3-strand floss unless otherwise indicated.

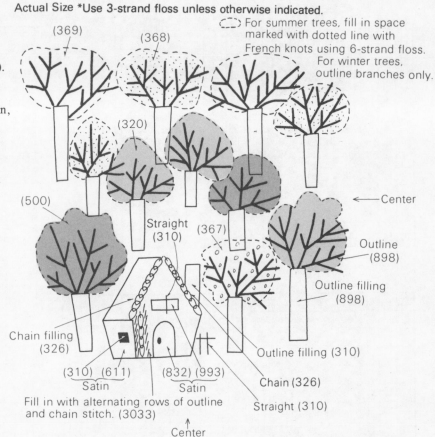

For summer trees, fill in space marked with dotted line with French knots using 6-strand floss. For winter trees, outline branches only.

(369) (368)

(320)

(500)

← Center

Straight (310)

(367)

Outline (898)

Outline filling (898)

Chain filling (326)

Outline filling (310)

(310) (611) (832) (993)
Satin   Satin

Chain (326)

Fill in with alternating rows of outline and chain stitch. (3033)

Straight (310)

↑ Center

HOUSES ON RED CANVAS

Shown on pages 22 & 23

Fabric: Red Java cloth, 35 mesh to 10 cm; 41 cm by 91 cm.
Thread: D.M.C cotton abroder: 3 skeins of Ash Gray (413).
Accessories: One pair bellpull accessories.
Finished size: 85 cm by 19 cm (embroidered area).
Gauge: One square of design equals one square mesh of fabric.
Directions: Cross-stitch as indicated for designs A through E using single-strand floss. Cross-stitch border design F as indicated in diagram E, reversing design for right side of fabric. Finish as shown in Finishing Diagram and attach bellpulls.

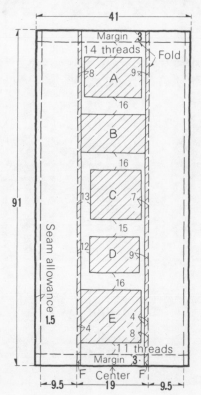

41

Margin 3

14 threads

Fold

8   A   9

16

B

16

13   C   7

15

12   D   9

16

E   4

4   8

11 threads

Margin 3

Seam allowance

1.5

91

F Center F

9.5   19   9.5

Finishing Hanging

(1) Fold embroidered cloth in half lengthwise with right sides facing. Sew seam allowance, turn inside out, and press with seam at center back.

19cm

(2) Fold back seam allowance at top and bottom of hanging and stitch to make casings.

3cm

A

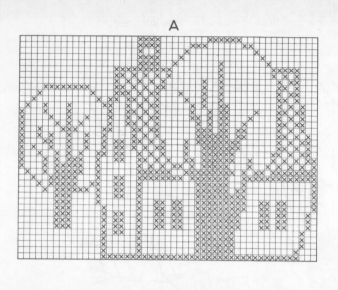

C

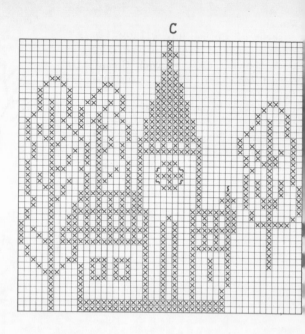

B

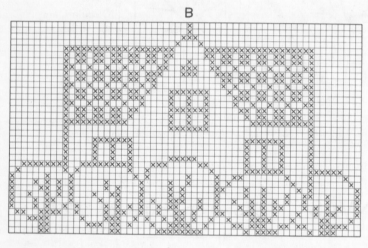

D

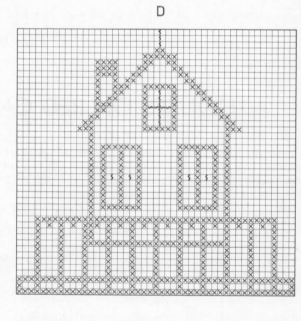

F   E

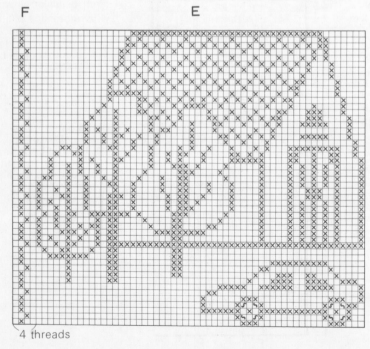

4 threads

⊠ = Cross-stitch with 413.
𝔖 = Holbein with 413.

56

NIGHT AND DAY Shown on page 19

Fabric: Suede cloth, 2 pieces, black and white, 21 cm square.
Thread: D.M.C 6-strand embroidery floss:
½ skein each of Sepia (3371), Drab (610), Peacock Green (991); small amount each of Royal Blue (796, 995), Sevres Blue (798), Scarlet (815, 498), Red Brown (918), Brilliant Green (701), Emerald Green (912), Smoke Gray (640) and Almond Green (502).

Frame: 15 cm square (inside measurements).
Finished size: Same size as frame.
Directions: Match centers of fabric and design, and transfer design to fabric. Embroider. Mount and frame.

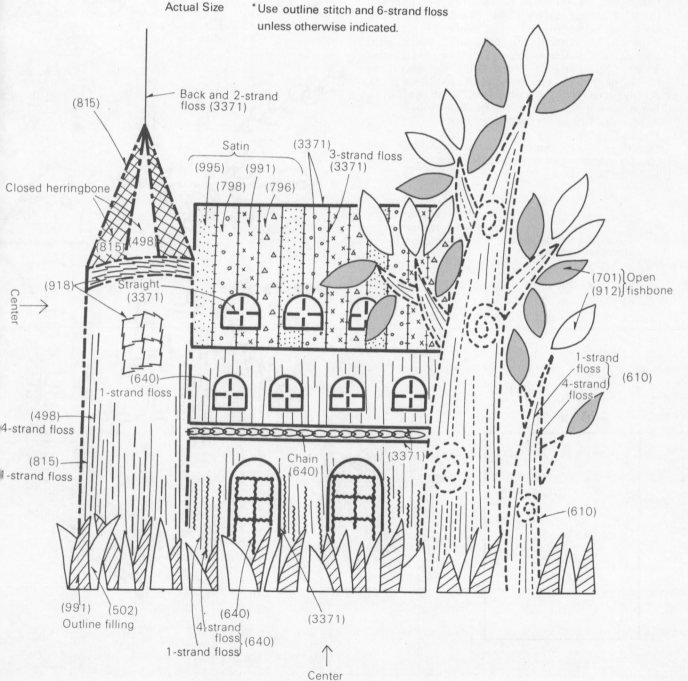

Actual Size   *Use outline stitch and 6-strand floss unless otherwise indicated.

BOUQUET WITH PURPLE RIBBON

Shown on pages 6 & 7

Fabric: Unbleached, heavyweight linen, 46 cm by 36 cm. Cotton for backing, 41 cm by 31 cm. Interfacing, 46 cm by 36 cm.

Thread: D.M.C 6-strand embroidery floss:
½ skein each of Brilliant Green (701, 702), Peacock Green (992, 993), Emerald Green (911), Geranium Red (892), Tangerine Yellow (740), Parma Violet (209), Buttercup Yellow (444), Canary Yellow (973), Lemom Yellow (307), Cerise (602, 603, 604), White; small amount each of Garnet Red (326), Plum (552), Parma Violet (208), Brilliant Green (700), Greenish Gray (597), Poppy (666), Fire Red (946), Laurel Green (988), Scarab Green (3347), Chestnut (950), Drab (611, 612), Forget-me-not Blue (809) and Sevres Blue (800).

Accessories: One pair bellpull accessories.

Finished size: 40 cm by 30 cm.

Directions: Match centers of fabric and design, and transfer design to fabric. Embroider. Finish as shown in Finishing Diagram.

Actual Size

*Use 6-strand floss unless otherwise indicated.

Flower stems: Outline stitch using 6-strand floss at bottom. 5-strand floss at center and 4-strand floss at ends.

Center

Straight (White)

Lazy daisy and 4-strand floss (950)

Chain stitch first, then pass through same color thread 3 times.
(604)
(603)
(602)

Satin (326)

(666)(892)(740)(9...

Outline filling

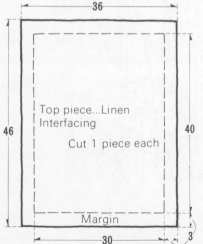

Top piece...Linen
Interfacing
Cut 1 piece each

36

46

40

30

3

Margin

*Cut 31cm by 41cm from lining fabric.

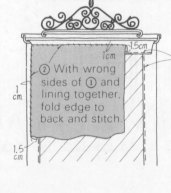

Finishing

② With wrong sides of ① and lining together, fold edge to back and stitch.

1cm

1.5cm

1 cm

1.5 cm

① Place interlining on wrong side of embroidered fabric. Turn margin to wrong side and baste. Insert bellpull attachments into margins at top and bottom.

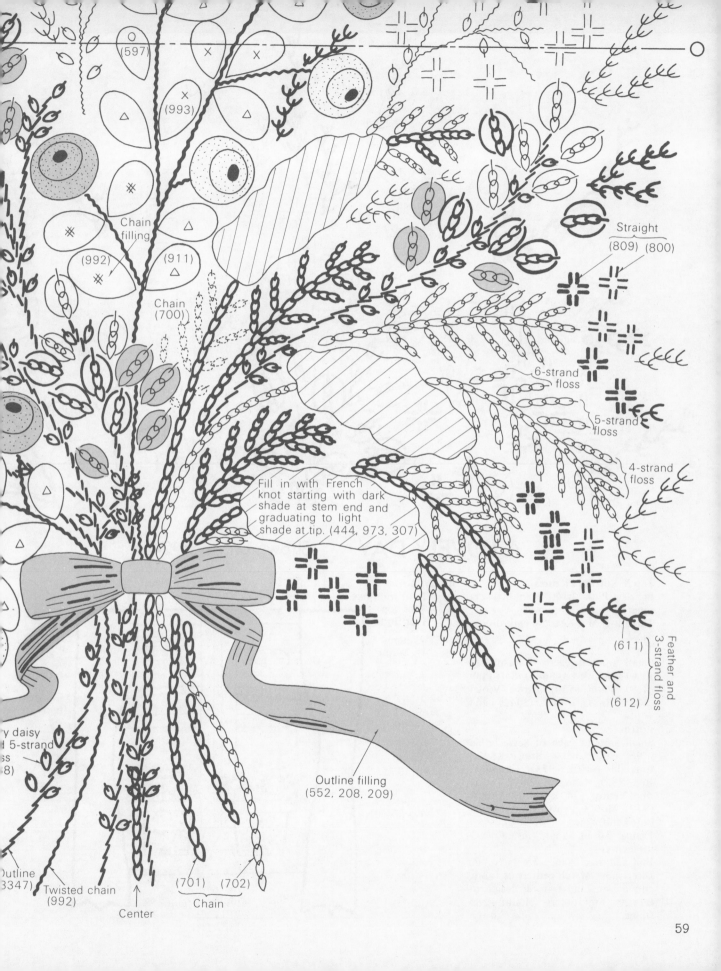

(597)

(993)

Chain
filling

(992)

(911)

Chain
(700)

Straight
(809) (800)

6-strand
floss

5-strand
floss

4-strand
floss

Fill in with French
knot starting with dark
shade at stem end and
graduating to light
shade at tip. (444, 973, 307)

(611)

Feather and
3-strand floss

(612)

y daisy
d 5-strand
ss
8)

Outline
3347)

Twisted chain
(992)

Center

(701) (702)

Chain

Outline filling
(552, 208, 209)

Straight (White)

Straight (800) (809)

Lazy daisy and 4-strand floss (950)

Twisted chain and 4-strand (950) floss

(933) X

(911) △

A LOVELY DAY Shown on page 24

Top & Bottom Pictures

Fabric: Pink Irish linen, 16 cm square.

Thread: D.M.C 6-strand embroidery floss:

Top

Small amount each of Raspberry Red (3685, 3688, 3689), Soft Pink (819), Plum (550), Parma Violet (208), Indian Red (3042) and White.

Bottm

Small amount each of Sevres Blue (798, 800), Beige Brown (840), Emerald Green (955), Geranium Red (892), Mahogany (301), Tangerine Yellow (743), Canary Yellow (972), Moss Green (937), Soft Pink (776) and White.

Frame: 10 cm square (inside measurements).

Finished size: Same size as frame.

Directions: Match centers of fabric and design, and transfer design to fabric. Embroider. Mount and frame.

Actual Size
*Use 3-strand floss.
[   ] for Top
(   ) for Bottom

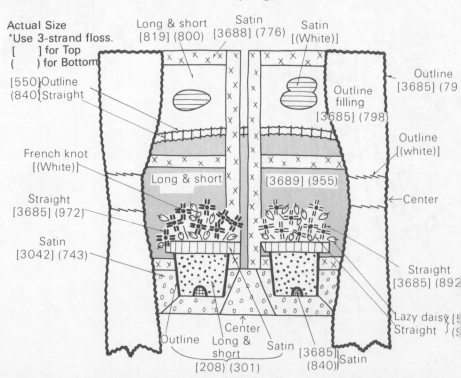

Long & short [819] (800)

Satin [3688] (776)

Satin [(White)]

Outline [3685] (79

[550] Outline
(840) Straight

Outline filling [3685] (798)

Outline [(white)]

French knot [(White)]

Long & short

[3689] (955)

Center

Straight [3685] (972)

Satin [3042] (743)

Straight [3685] (892

Outline   Long &   Satin
          short
[208] (301)

Center

[3685] (840) Satin

Lazy daisy [5
Straight   (9

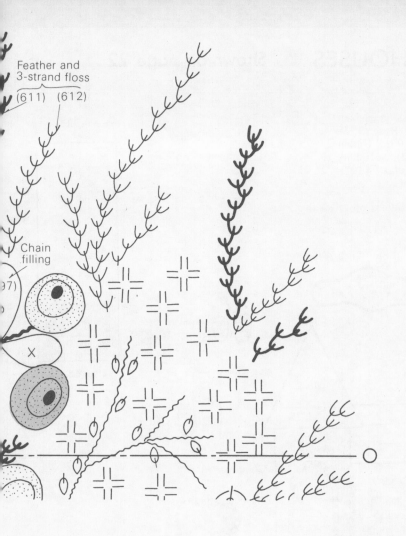

Feather and
3-strand floss
(611) (612)

Chain
filling
(97)

X

Center Picture

Fabric: Cream Irish linen, 16 cm square.
Thread: D.M.C 6-strand embroidery floss:
Center
Small amount each of Golden Yellow (782),
Saffron (725), Beige Brown (840), Cornflower
Blue (792), Laurel Green (988), Garnet Red
(326) and Geranium Red (948).
Frame: 10 cm square (inside measurements).
Finished size: Same size as frame.
Directions: Match centers of fabric and design,
and transfer design to fabric. Embroider. Mount
and frame.

Actual Size
*Use 3-strand floss.
Use satin stitch unless
otherwise indicated.

(782)

French knot
(840)

(948)

(792)

(725)

Cross (988)

Couched trellis
Crossing thread (725)
Tacking thread (988)

Center →

(725)
(326)
(988)

Outline

(326)

Cross (792)

Center

BLUE AND RED HOUSES

Shown on page 22

Fabric: Cotton, 49 cm by 37 cm.
Thread: D.M.C 6-strand embroidery floss:
1 skein each of Brilliant Green (702, 703); ½ skein each of
Flame Red (606), Brilliant Green (701), Peony Rose (957),
White; small amount each of Royal Blue (995, 996), Umber
(435), Brilliant Green (699, 700), Cerise (602), Soft Pink
(776, 899), Canary Yellow (973), Lemon Yellow (307),

*Cut back piece same size
as front.
Don't embroider on back.

Front

A

Actual Size

*Use 3-strand floss and satin stitch unless otherwise
indicated.

18.5

Margin

4

Seam allowance

Embroider
area A

49

4

46

Embroider
area B

4

14.5

2

1.5

Fill in with lazy daisy
(702)

German knot
(606)

Chain filling (White)

Closed herringbone
Outline (995)

Back (422)

Straight
(422)

(307)

Chain (436)

(362)

Long & short (white)

(435)

Fill in with
french knot
(700)

(700)

Macramé (703)

Lazy
daisy

(703)

Outline

Straight
(703)

(606)

Outline
(701)

(701)

(892) } Double
(776) } lazy daisy

(973)

(892)

Fill in with
french knot

(703)

(973)

(703) } Fill in with
(702) } lazy daisy

(703) } Chain
(702) }

Outline(435)

(435)

French knot (973)

(899)

(957)

(702)

Outline (702)

Center

62

Tangerine Yellow (742), Umber (436, 739), Hazel-nut Brown (422), Sevres Blue (800) and Geranium Red (892).
Accessories: One pair bellpull accessories.
Finished size: Refer to diagram.
Directions: Match centers of fabric and design, and transfer design to fabric. Embroider. Finish as shown in Finishing Diagram.

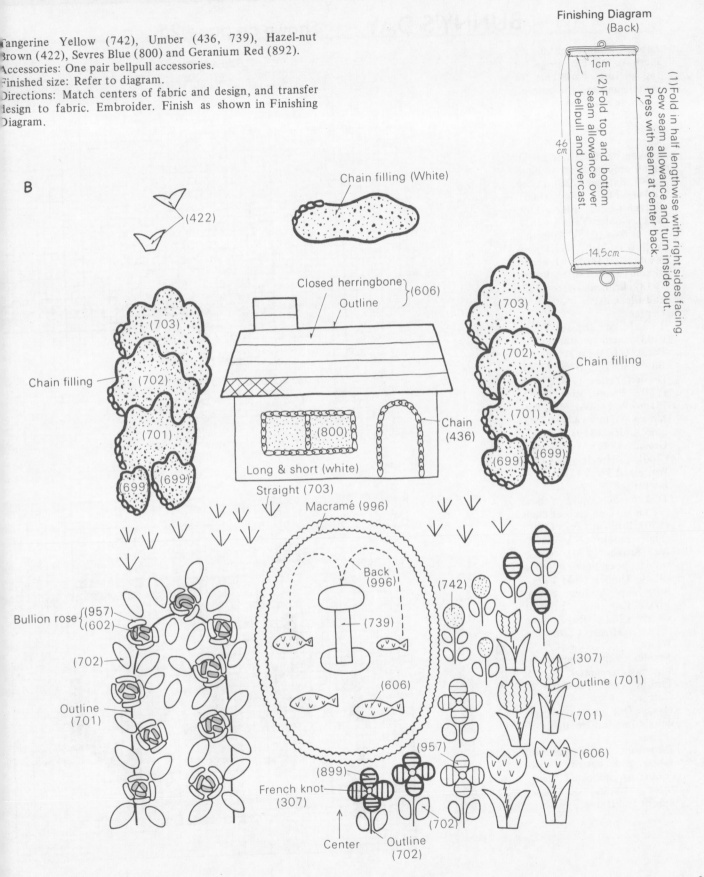

B

(422)

Chain filling (White)

Closed herringbone
Outline } (606)

(703)

(703)

Chain filling

(702)

(702)

Chain filling

(701)

(701)

(800)

Chain (436)

Long & short (white)

(699)

(699)

(699)

(699)

Straight (703)

Macramé (996)

Back (996)

(742)

Bullion rose {(957)
(602)}

(739)

(307)

(702)

Outline (701)

Outline (701)

(701)

(606)

(606)

(957)

(899)

French knot (307)

Center

Outline (702)

(702)

Finishing Diagram
(Back)

1cm

46 cm

14.5cm

(2)Fold top and bottom seam allowance over bellpull and overcast.

(1)Fold in half lengthwise with right sides facing. Sew seam allowance and turn inside out. Press with seam at center back.

BUNNY'S DAY   Shown on page 25

Fabric: Indian cloth, 52 mesh to 10 cm; beige for top picture, dark blue for center, and red for bottom, 18 cm square each.

Thread: D.M.C 6-strand embroidery floss:

Top

1 skein of Chestnut (407); small amount each of Plum (550), Saffron (726), Cerise (604), Flame Red (606), Forget-me-not Blue (809, 824), Golden Yellow (783), Royal Blue (996), Tangerine Yellow (740), Buttercup Yellow (444), Emerald Green (911), Coffee Brown (938), Brilliant Green (703) and Black (310).

Center

1 skein of Brilliant Green (703); small amount each of Cerise (603), Forget-me-not Blue (308), Saffron (726), Golden Yellow (780), Plum (550), Peony Rose (957), Flame Red (606, 608), Buttercup Yellow (444), Pistachio Green (319), Emerald Green (911), Mahogany (300), Coffee Brown (938), White and Black (310).

Bottm

1 skein of Golden Yellow (783); ½ skein each of Plum (550), Brilliant Green (700); small amount each of Coffee Brown (898), Cerise (604), Forget-me-not Blue (824), Umber Gold (975), Buttercup Yellow (444), Flame Red (606), Brilliant Green (703), Royal Blue (996), Saffron (726) and White.

Frames: 12 cm square (inside measurements).

Finished size: Same size as frames.

Gauge: One square of design equals one square mesh of fabric.

Directions: Match centers of fabric and design. Crossstitch as indicated using three strands of floss. Mount and frame.

	Top	Center
Ⓞ	606	606
⊙	444	444
▽	911	319
▼	911	606
Ⓩ	911	White
●	310	310
+	606	726
·	996	911
▨	740	608
◪	604	550
△	824	606

▨ =Holbein stitch with 938
( )=Top
[ ]=Center

Top and Center

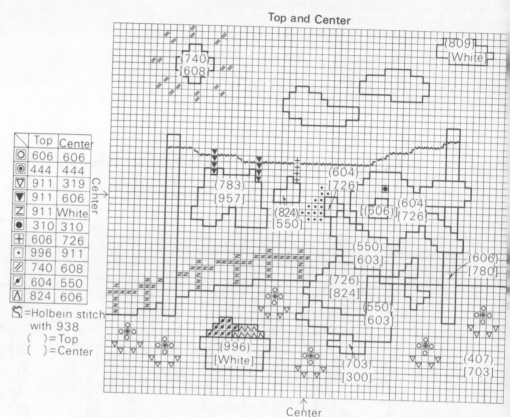

Center

Bottom

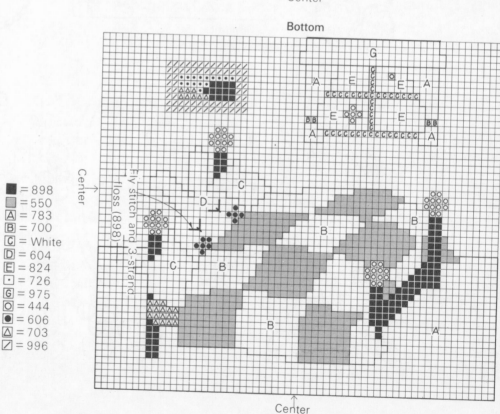

■ = 898
▨ = 550
Ⓐ = 783
Ⓑ = 700
Ⓒ = White
Ⓓ = 604
Ⓔ = 824
· = 726
Ⓖ = 975
Ⓞ = 444
● = 606
△ = 703
◪ = 996

Fly stitch and 3-strand floss (898)

Center

MADEMOISELLE Shown on page 30

Fabric: Beige Indian cloth, 52 mesh to 10 cm; 40 cm by 30 cm.

Thread: D.M.C 6-strand embroidery floss:

1 skein of Azure Blue (3325); ½ skein of Cornflower Blue (793); small amount each of Cerise (600, 604), Soft Pink (899), Episcopal Purple (718), Raspberry Red (3688), Parakeet Green (904), Laurel Green (988), Scarab Green (3348), Geranium Pink (894), Cornflower Blue (792), Saffron (726), Light Yellow (3078), Beaver Gray (647) and Magenta Rose (963).

Finished size: 30 cm by 20 cm (size of display panel).

Gauge: One square of design equals one square mesh of fabric.

Directions: Match centers of fabric and design. Cross-stitch using three strands of floss. Mount onto display panel.

- ⊡ =3348
- ☒ = 988
- Ⅴ = 793
- ⊠ =894
- ⊚ =904
- △ = 792
- A =600
- B =899
- ⬭ =Holbein stitch and 2-strand floss with 647
- C = 604
- D =3688
- ▲ =3325
- ⊞ = 726
- ⊕ = 3078
- ⊕ = 647
- ⊥ = 718
- O = 963

Center

Center

DUCKS AND WINDMILL   Shown on page 32, left

Fabric: Blue Indian cloth, 52 mesh to 10 cm; 32 cm by 29 cm. Blue cotton broadcloth, 23 cm by 16 cm. Fusible interfacing, 21 cm by 14 cm.

Thread: D.M.C 6-strand embridery floss: 1½ skeins each of Royal Blue (996), Laures Green (988); 1 skein each of Cardinal Red (347), Emerald Green (911); ½ skein of white; small amount each of Golden Yellow (782), Red Brown (918), Mahogany (301), Pistachio Green (367), Drab (611), Brilliant Green (704), Moss Green (936), Saffron (727), Royal Blue (796), Canary Yellow (972) and Black (310).

Accessories: One pair bellpull accessories.
Finished size: Refer to diagram.
Gauge: One square of design equals one square mesh of fabric.

Directions: Cross-stitch as indicated using three strands of floss unless otherwise indicated. Finish as shown in Finishing Diagram.

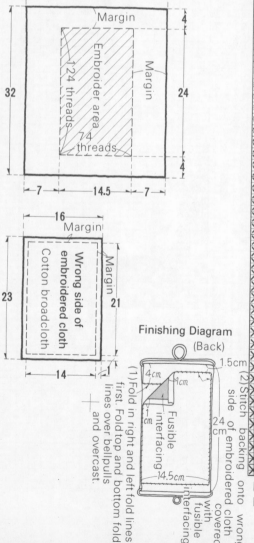

| ▨ =996 | B =988 | ▦ =911 | ⊙ =White | ● =310 | △ =972 | Ⅲ =796 | ∅ =727 | ☒ | 347 (One square of design equals two square meshes of fabric) 6-strand floss |
| ⊥ =936 | U =704 | ⊞ =301 | ▲ =367 | ∨ =611 | ✛ =918 | A =782 |

FLOWER FAIRY

Shown on page 33

Fabric: Beige Oxford cloth, 72 mesh to 10 cm; 28 cm by 23 cm. Cotton broadcloth for lining, 25 cm by 21 cm.
Thread: D.M.C 6-strand embroidery floss:
½ skein each of Sky Blue (518), Soft Pink (776, 818), Cerise (604), Raspberry Red (3689); small amount each of Cerise (601), Episcopal Purple (718), Smoke Gray (640,642), Copper Green (833), Sky Blue (517), Parma Violet (208), Black (310) and White.

Accessories: One pair bellpull accessories.
Finished size: Refer to diagram.
Directions: Match centers of fabric and design, and transfer design to fabric. Finish as shown in Finishing Diagram.

Actual Size   *Use 4-strand floss and chain filling stitch unless otherwise indicated.

Top piece

Finishing Diagram
(Back)

(1)Fold back seam allowance of embroidered cloth, fold again at fold line, covering bellpulls at top and bottom.
(2)Fold in seam allowance of backing and overcast.

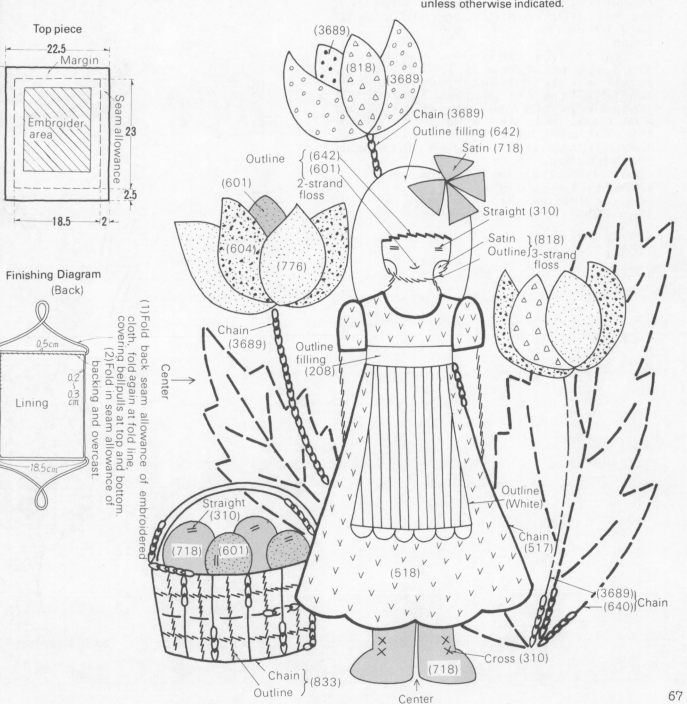

67

GIRL GATHERING FLOWERS

Shown on page 34

Fabric: Off-white Irish linen, 40 cm by 36 cm; two pieces.
Thread: D.M.C 6-strands embroidery floss:

Top

2 skeins of Geranium Red (754); 1 skein each of Tangerine
Yellow (740, 741); ½ skein each of Sevres Blue (798),
Saffron (727), Brilliant Green (702, 703), Mahogany (402);
small amount each of Flame Red (608), Cerise (602, 604),
Chestnut (950), Morocco Red (760), Geranium Pink (891),
Red Brown (918), Umber (433), Sepia (3371), Emerald
Green (911) and White.

Bottom

1½ skeins of Soft Pink (818); 1 skein each of Soft Pink (776,
899); ½ skein each of Sevres Blue (798), Saffron (727),
Emerald Green (911, 912), Geranium Pink (891), Peony
Rose (957), Umber Gold (976); small amount each of
Tangerine Yellow (743), Canary Yellow (972), Peony Rose
(956), Chestnut (950), Morocco Red (760, 761), Umber
Gold (975), Lemon Yellow (307), Emerald Green (954),
Scarlet (815), Sepia (3371), Brilliant Green (703), Geranium
Red (948) and White.

Frames: 34 cm by 29.5 cm (inside measurements).

Finished size: Same size as frame.

Directions: Match centers of fabric and design, and transfer
design to fabric. Embroider. Mount and frame.

Actual Size

* Use 3-strand floss unless otherwise indicated.
( ) for Bottom [ ] for Top

Long & short

a = (818) [754]
b = (776) [471]
c = (899) [740]
d = (957) [740]
e = (956) [608] } 2-strand floss

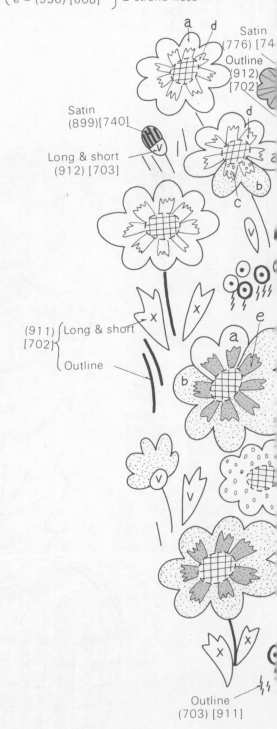

Satin (776) [74
Outline (912) [702]

Satin (899) [740]

Long & short (912) [703]

(911) [702] { Long & short
Outline

Outline (703) [911]

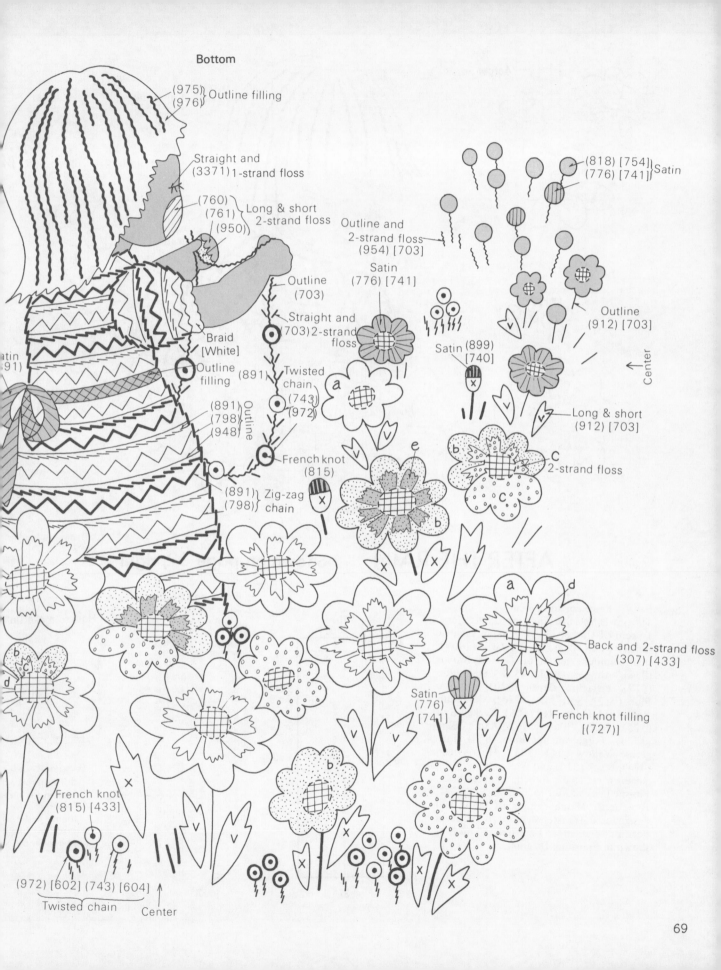

Bottom

(975) Outline filling
(976)

Straight and
(3371) 1-strand floss

(760) Long & short
(761) 2-strand floss
(950)

Outline and
2-strand floss
(954) [703]

Satin
(776) [741]

(818) [754] Satin
(776) [741]

Outline
(703)

Straight and
(703) 2-strand
floss

Satin (899)
[740]

Outline
(912) [703]

Braid
[White]

atin
91]

Outline
filling

Outline (891)
filling

Twisted
chain
(743)
(972)

Long & short
(912) [703]

(891) Outline
(798)
(948)

a

e

b C
2-strand floss

C

French knot
(815)

b

(891) Zig-zag
(798) chain

X

Back and 2-strand floss
(307) [433]

a d

b
C
d

Satin
(776)
[741]

b

Satin
(776)
[741]

X

C

French knot filling
[(727)]

French knot
(815) [433]

V

X

V

b

C

(972) [602] (743) [604]
Twisted chain   Center

Center

69

Top
Actual Size

[402])
[918]) Outline filling

[3371]) Straight and
[891]) 1-strand floss

Long & short
and 2-strand {[754]}
floss   {[760]}

Cross and
2-strand
floss [891]
Cable chain
Outline {[798]}

French knot
[3371]

Braid
(White)

[604] [602]
Twisted chain

[950]

[950]
2-strand
floss

AFTER THE RAIN   Shown on page 32, right

Fabric: Beige cotton, 56 cm by 41 cm.
Thread: D.M.C 6-strand embroidery floss:
1 skein of Umber (738); ½ skein each of
Garnet Red (309), Emerald Green (909);
small amount each of Coffee Brown
(938), Umber (433, 435), Sky Blue
(517), Pistachio Green (320), Antique
Blue (932), Soft Pink (776), Geranium
Red (351), Flame Red (606), Turkey Red
(321), Royal Blue (796), Azure Blue
(3325), Forget-me-not Blue (828), Tangerine Yellow (741, 743), Moss Green
(471), Black (310) and White.
Accessories: One pair bellpull accessories.
Finished size: Refer to diagram.
Directions: Match centers of fabric and
design, and transfer designs to fabric in
positions indicated. Embroider. Finish as
shown in Finishing Diagram.

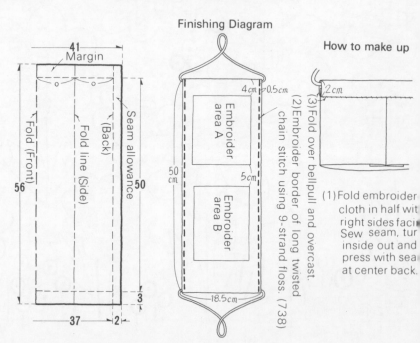

Finishing Diagram

How to make up

(1) Fold embroider
cloth in half wit
right sides faci
Sew seam, tur
inside out and
press with sea
at center back.

A Actual Size

*Use 3-strand floss unless otherwise indicated.

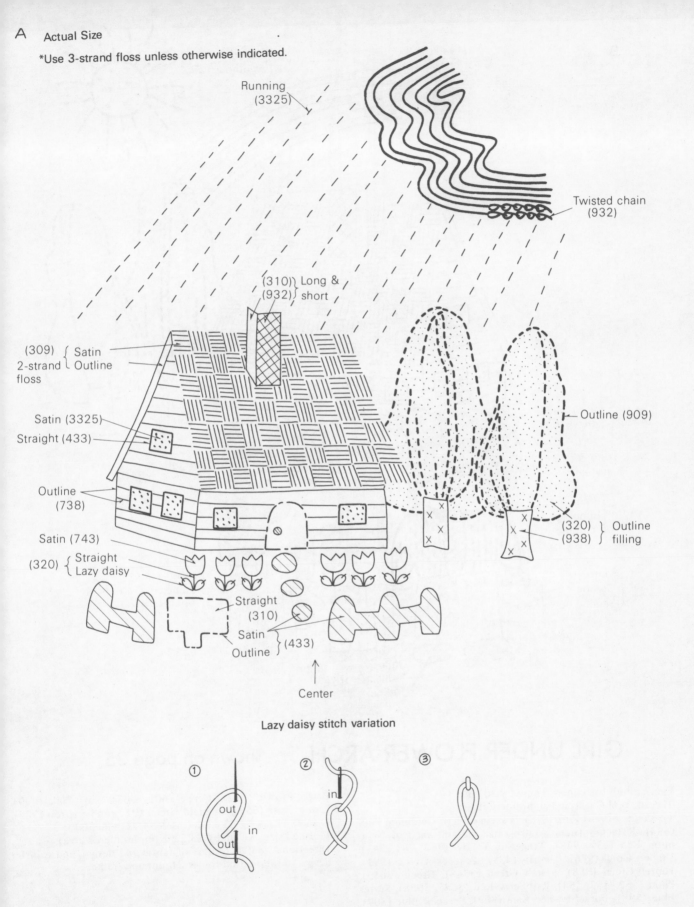

Running (3325)

Twisted chain (932)

(310) Long &
(932) short

(309) { Satin
2-strand { Outline
floss

Satin (3325)
Straight (433)

Outline (738)

Satin (743)

(320) { Straight
Lazy daisy

Outline (909)

(320) } Outline
(938) } filling

Straight (310)

Satin } (433)
Outline

Center

Lazy daisy stitch variation

① out out in

② in

③

71

B

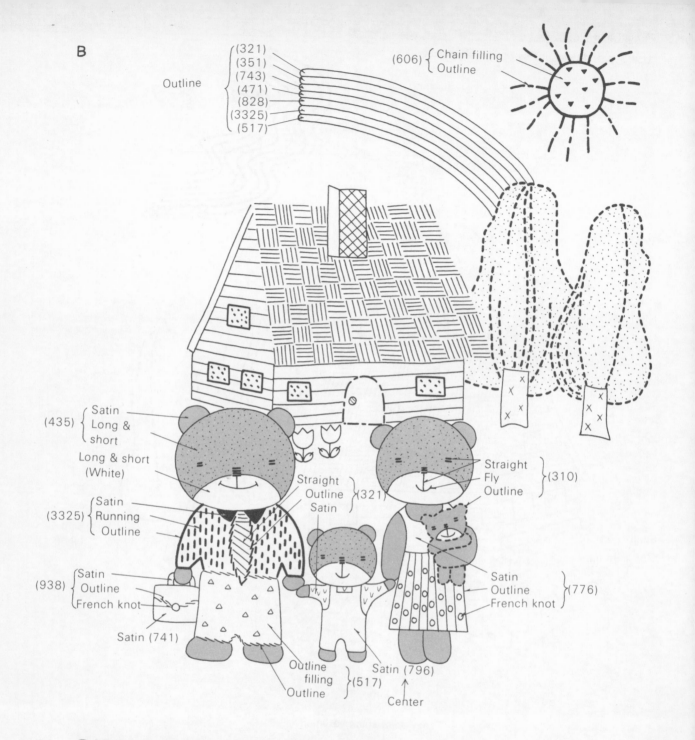

(321)
(351)
(743)
(471) Outline
(828)
(3325)
(517)

(606) { Chain filling / Outline

(435) { Satin / Long & short
Long & short (White)
(3325) { Satin / Running / Outline
Straight / Outline / Satin
(321)
Straight / Fly / Outline
(310)
(938) { Satin / Outline / French knot
Satin (741)
Satin / Outline / French knot
(776)
Outline / filling / Outline
(517)
Satin (796)
Center

GIRL UNDER FLOWER ARCH   Shown on page 35

Fabric: Pink Irish linen, 37 cm by 30 cm.
Thread: D.M.C 6-strand embroidery floss:
1½ skeins of Soft Pink (818); ½ skein each of Geranium Pink (894), Pistachio Green (320); small amount each of Geranium Red (351, 948), Tangerine Yellow (740, 741, 743), Umber Gold (976), Umber (433), Peacock Green (991), Laurel Green (988), Scarab Green (3348), Green (3053), Plum (552, 553, 554), Raspberry Red (3685, 3688), Sevres Blue (798), Forget-me-not Blue (809), Peacock Blue (807),

Beige Brown (842), Cerise (601, 603), Soft Pink (899), Peony Rose (957), Emerald Green (912) and Saffron (725).
Frame: 41 cm by 33.5 cm (inside measurements).
Finished size: 31 cm by 23.5 cm (embroidered area).
Directions: Match centers of fabric and design, and transfer design to fabric. Embroider. Mount and frame.

Actual Size

* Use 3-strand floss and long & short stitch unless otherwise indicated.

Outline (988)

a

c

o

x

German knot and (725)6-strand floss

O = 991
X = 988
△ = 320
□ = 3053

Closed herringbone (807)

Outline (725)

Chain filling (743)

(3688)

c

Chain filling (725)

Outline filling (743)

French knot (807)

e

f

Outline (976) 2 Join to (433) 1 3-strand floss

(3685)

b

German knot and 6-strand (743) floss

Long & short (948)

Double lazy daisy (912)

(899)

f

a

(552)

Satin (988)

Center

Outline (988)

f

e

(842)

Outline (809) 2-strand floss

Satin (798)

Outline filling (433)

Satin (320)

f

f

e

(957)

Outline (3348)

e

(601)

Satin (320)

(603)

e

f

German knot and 6-strand floss (740)

(553) (554)

Satin

f

Random cross and 1-strand floss (809)

Outline (976)

French knot (741)

Satin (3348)

e

Outline (912)

Outline (912)

(833)

Satin (894)

Satin (320)

Outline (3348)

Outline (320)

Satin (988)

(818)

(351)

(894)

Satin (320)

Center

COBBLESTONE STREET

Shown on pages 14 & 15

Fabric: Unbleached linen, 49 cm by 34 cm.
Thread: D.M.C 6-strand embroidery floss:
1½ skeins of Umber Gold (977); ½ skein each of Pistachio Green (319, 367), Parakeet Green (904), Laurel Green (988), Scarab Green (3347), Moss Green (937, 469, 471), Scarlet (815, 498), Fire Red (900, 947), Canary Yellow (971), Tangerine Yellow (740), Flame Red (606), Beaver Gray (646), Almond Green (502), Beige Brown (841), Umber (435, 738, 739), Umber Gold (975), Antique Gray (535) and Coffee Brown (898); small amount each of Faded Pink (224), Dull Mouve (778), Saffron (726), Terra-cotta (355), Red Brown (920), Brilliant Green (701), Emerald Green (911), Peacock Green (993), Plum (552), Parma Violet (209), Garnet Red (326), Mahogany (300), Umber (433), Sky Blue (518), Soft Pink (899), Episcopal Purple (718), Flame Red (608), Geranium Pink (891) and Black (310).
Finished size: 39 cm by 24 cm.
Directions: Match centers of fabric and design, and transfer design to fabric. Mount onto panel.

Actual Size

*Use 4-strand floss and satin stitch unless otherwise indicated.

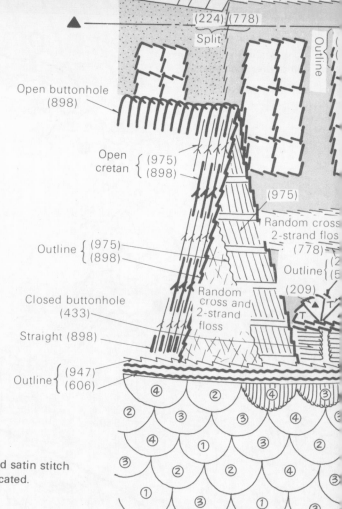

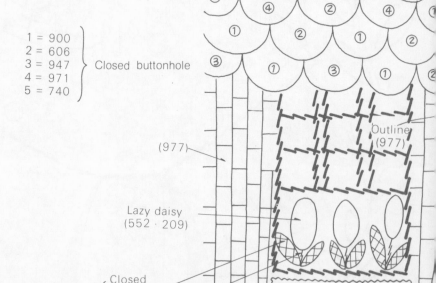

Open creten stitch

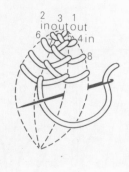

1 = 900
2 = 606
3 = 947 } Closed buttonhole
4 = 971
5 = 740

Split stitch

Split thread as you embroider.

Open cretan

Random cross and 2-strand (993) floss

Chain filling

(975)
(898)

(347)
(988)
(904)

Back (701)

French knot (891)

(899)
(718)

(502) } Outline
(701) } filling

plit 88)

Split and 2-strand floss (977)

Outline filling (518)

Straight (518)

Outline filling

(518)

Straight (518)

Center

Outline (739)

Outline filling

Closed herringbone

(911)

(993)

Back (535)

(993) (718)

Straight (535)

French knot (726)

Straight (701)

Lazy daisy (891)

Outline { (535)
          { (726)

Random cross and 2-strand (726) floss

Split (778)

Closed herringbone (209)

Long & short

Outline filling (224)

Outline { (535)
          { (433)

(435)

(841)

(975)

△

Outline (898)

Outline (977)

Fill in with zig-zag stitch (738)

Split and 2-strand (977) floss

(718)
(891)
(899)
(904)
Lazy daisy } 904
Outline

Outline (646)(310) and 3-strand floss

Outline (535)

(310) 3-strand floss

Outline (535)

Center

Outline (738)

FLORIST Shown on page 26

Fabric: Heavyweight Irish linen, 23 cm square.
Thread: D.M.C 6-strand embroidery floss:
1½ skeins of Royal Blue (797); ½ skein of White; small amount each of Plum (553), Geranium Red (350), Canary Yellow (971), Tangerine Yellow (741), Brilliant Green (699, 703), Emerald Green (911, 912), Coffee Brown (898), Flame Red (606), Cerise (601), Raspberry Red (3685), Episcopal Purple (718), Soft Pink (899), Peony Rose (957), Yellow Green (732) and Geranium Pink (891).

Frame: 17 cm square (inside measurements).
Finished size: Same size as frame.
Directions: Match centers of fabric and design, and transfer design to fabric. Embroider. Mount and frame.

Actual Size
* Use 3-strand floss unless otherwise indicated.

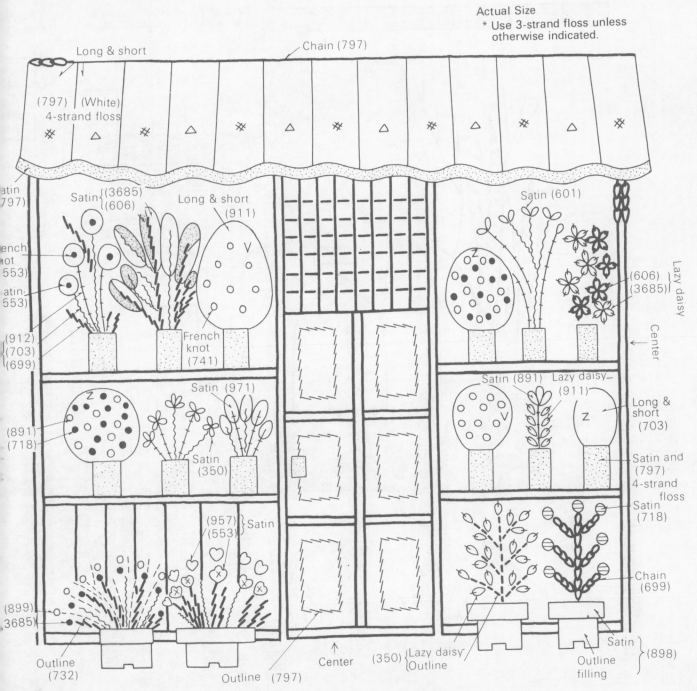

77

MORNING AND EVENING

Shown on page 31

Fabric: Coarse, heavyweight linen, 50 cm by 47 cm each.
Morning: Unbleached. Evening: Dark blue.
Thread: D.M.C 6-strand embroidery floss:
Morning
1½ skeins of Geranium Red (892); 1 skein each of Canary
Yellow (971), Cerise (602), Episcopal Purple (718), Peacock
Green (993), Antique Blue (932), Forget-me-not Blue (824);

½ skein each of Flame Red (606), Poppy (666), Cerise
603), Peacock Green (991, 992), Emerald Green (9
Parma Violet (208), Antique Blue (931), Indigo (336, 8
Peacock Blue (807) and Umber (436); small amount ea
Cornflower Blue (794), Parma Violet (209), Indigo
312, 334), Antique Blue (930), Ash Gray (415), Fo
me-not Blue (809), Peacock Blue (806) and White.

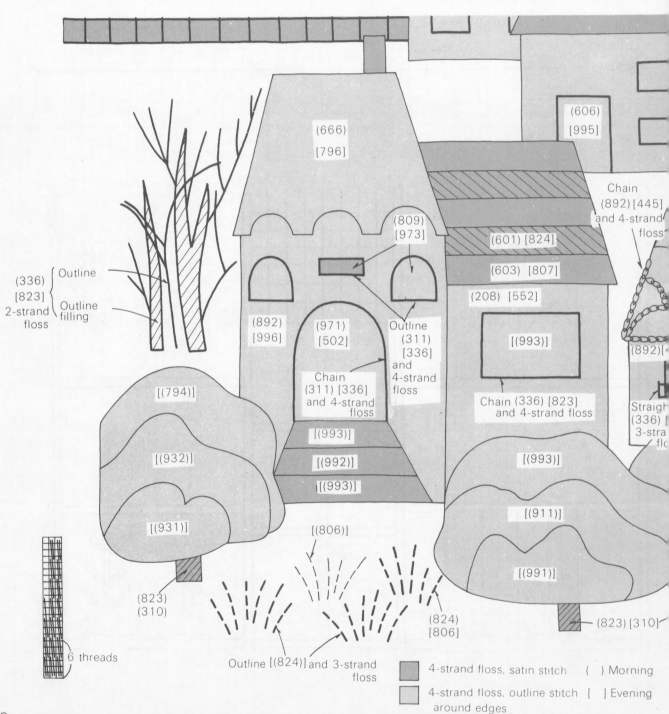

(336) [823] 2-strand floss { Outline / Outline filling

(666) [796]

(809) [973]

(606) [995]

Chain (892) [445] and 4-strand floss

(601) [824]

(603) [807]

(208) [552]

Outline (311) [336] and 4-strand floss

(892) [996]

(971) [502]

[(993)]

Chain (311) [336] and 4-strand floss

[(993)]

[(992)]

[(993)]

[(794)]

[(932)]

[(931)]

Chain (336) [823] and 4-strand floss

[(993)]

[(911)]

[(991)]

Straigh (336) [3-stra fl

(892)[

6 threads

(823) (310)

[(806)]

(824) [806]

(823) [310]

Outline [(824)] and 3-strand floss

4-strand floss, satin stitch ( ) Morning

4-strand floss, outline stitch [ ] Evening around edges

78

Evening

1½ skeins of Royal Blue (996), 1 skein each of Peacock Blue (806, 807), Forget-me-not Blue (824), Almond Green (502), Episcopal Purple (718), Peacock Green (993), Antique Blue (932); ½ skein each of Royal Blue (776, 995), Plum (552), Peacock Green (991, 992), Emerald Green (911), Antique Blue (931), Umber (433); small amount each of Parma Violet (208), Cornflower Blue (794), Antique Blue (930), Indigo (312, 336, 823), Ash Grey (415), Canary Yellow (973), Lemon Yellow (445), Ivy Green (550), White and Black (310).

Frame: 40 cm by 37 cm (inside measurements).
Finished size: Same size as frame.
Directions: Match centers of fabric and design, and transfer design to fabric. Embroider. Mount and frame.

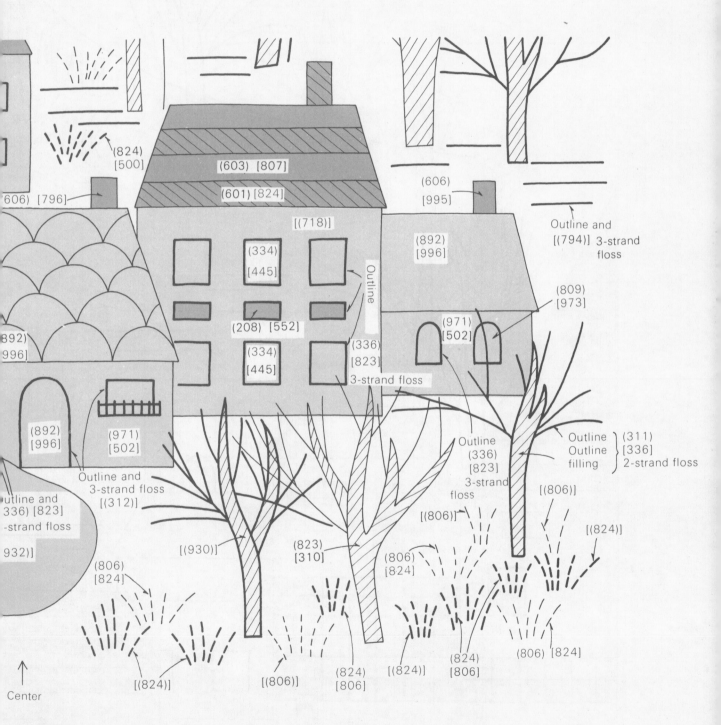

79

Outline
Outline } [(931)]
filling   2-strand floss

[(932)]

German knot filling and
[992] 6-strand floss

[(824)]

(824)
[806]

Germa
knot f
[(932)
6-st

[(993)]

Outline [(932)]
and 3-strand
floss

(336)
[823]

(824)
[500]

(602)
[806]

(806)
[500]

(971) [995]

(606) [502]

(602)
[806]

(892)
[996]

Outline and
[(718)]   (336)
           [823]
(208)   3-strand floss
[552]

(809) [973]

(601) [807]

(603) [824]

(208)
[552]

(809)
[973]

(606)
[995]

Outline and
[(336)]
3-strand floss

[(718)]

Outline filling
and[(932)]
2-strand floss

[(718)]

(209)
[208]

Center →

Outline and
[(336)]3-strand
floss

(809)
[973]

(606) [995]

(971) [502]

(892)
[996]

(334)
[445]

Outline [(White)]
and 4-strand floss

[(415)]

(606)
[796]

Outline (336)
[823]
and 3-strand floss

Outline and 3-strand
[336]floss

80

Outline [(993)] and 4-strand floss

[(992)]
[(993)] } Straight and 3-strand floss

[(824)]
[(807)]

[(992)]
[(993)]

German knot filling and 6-strand floss [(911)]

French knot filling and 4-strand floss [(991)]

[(824)]

(823)
[310]

(602)
[806]

Outline filling and

(436)[433]

4-strand floss

(602)
[806]

[(718)]

German knot filling and 6-strand floss

[(932)]

[(932)]

(208)
[552]

(602)
[806]

Outline and
(311)
[336]
3-strand
floss

[(911)]

[(931)]

[(991)]

(892) [995]

(606) [996]

(602)
[806]

(806) [824]

[(932)]

[(794)] } Outline
(806) } and
[824] } 3-strand
[(824)] } floss

(892)
[996]

Outline and
[(336)]
3-strand
floss

(806)
[500]

(823)
[310]

(823)
[310]

(931)
[336]

81

SPRING WIND

Shown on page 23

Fabric: Heavyweight linen, 25 cm by 73 cm.
Thread: D.M.C 6-strand embroidery floss:
½ skein each of Cerise (601), Episcopal Purple (718), Brilliant Green (699, 701), Green (3051), Scarab Green (3347); small amount each of Emerald Green (913, 954), Brilliant Green (703), Peacock Green (991, 992), Laurel Green (986, 988), Parakeet Green (904), Scarab Green (3348), Moss Green (936), Royal Blue (996), Geranium Red (352), Tangerine Yellow (740), Poppy (666), Greenish Gray (597), Sevres Blue (798), Parma Violet (209), Soft Pink (776), Cerise (603), Drab (610), Coffee Brown (938) and White.
Finished size: Refer to diagram.
Directions: Transfer design to fabric and embroider. Finish as shown in Finishing Diagram.

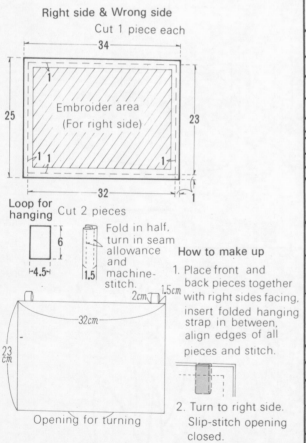

Right side & Wrong side
Cut 1 piece each

34

1

Embroider area
(For right side)

25   23

1 1   1

32

1

Loop for hanging Cut 2 pieces

6

4.5

1.5

Fold in half, turn in seam allowance and machine-stitch.

1.5cm

2cm   1.5cm

32cm

23 cm

Opening for turning

How to make up

1. Place front and back pieces together with right sides facing, insert folded hanging strap in between, align edges of all pieces and stitch.

2. Turn to right side. Slip-stitch opening closed.

Actual Size

*Use 4-strand floss.

———— = (3051)	∿∿∿ = (986)	∼∼∼ = (992)
∼∼ = (669)	++++ = (904)	—·— = (913)
⫫⫫ = (701)	—·—· = (3347)	------ = (209)
•—•—• = (936)	- - - - = (703)	+-+-+ = (988)
— — = (991)	∿∿∿ = (798)	∼∼ = (996)

Outline

(3347)

(988)

Chain filling (601)

Straight (699) and 3-strand fl[...]

French knot and 3-strand fl[...]
(209, 603, 601, 718,
  352, 740, 701, 666)

82

= (954)

= (3348)

Long & short

(White)

(White)

Long & short

(996)

Long & short

(01)

(913)

Satin
(938)

Chain
(610) (3051)

(718)

Satin

(601)

Chain filling

(601)

(718)

(699)

(986)

Satin
(603)
(776)

(776)

Outline and 2-strand floss
(3051, 701)

MOSQUES Shown on page 21

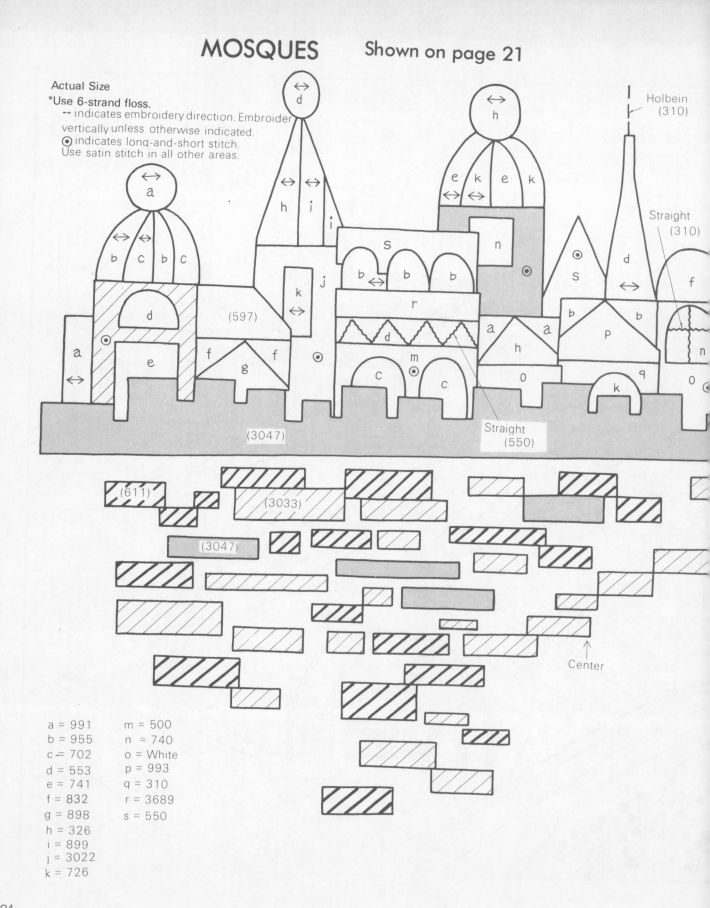

Actual Size

*Use 6-strand floss.

↔ indicates embroidery direction. Embroider vertically unless otherwise indicated.

⊙ indicates long-and-short stitch.

Use satin stitch in all other areas.

Holbein (310)

Straight (310)

Straight (550)

(597)

(3047)

(611)

(3033)

(3047)

Center

a = 991
b = 955
c = 702
d = 553
e = 741
f = 832
g = 898
h = 326
i = 899
j = 3022
k = 726

m = 500
n = 740
o = White
p = 993
q = 310
r = 3689
s = 550

Fabric: Cream congress canvas, 70 mesh to 10 cm; 29 cm by 36 cm.
Thread: D.M.C 6-strand embroidery floss:
2 skeins of Drab (611); 1½ skeins of Beige (3047); 1 skein of Dark Brown (3033); small amount each of Plum (550, 553), Peacock Green (991, 993), Emerald Green (955), Brilliant Green (702), Ivy Green (500), Tangerine Yellow (740, 741), Saffron (726), Copper Green (832), Coffee Brown (898),

Beige (3022), Garnet Red (326), Soft Pink (899), Raspberry Red (3689), Greenish Gray (597), White and Black (310).
Frame: 23 cm by 29.5 cm (inside measurements).
Finished size: Same size as frame.
Directions: Match centers of fabric and design, and transfer design to fabric. Embroider to fill in blocks of color as shown. Mount and frame.

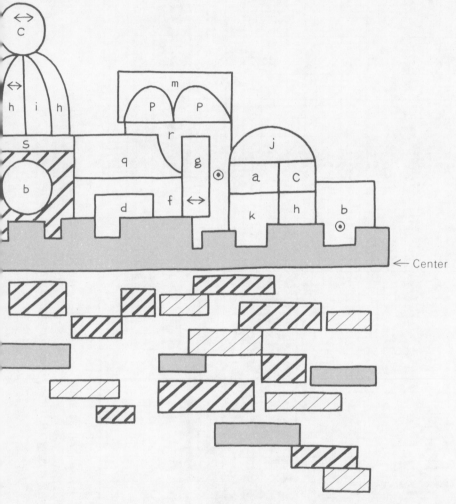

← Center

TREES Shown on page 18

Fabric: Beige Indian cloth, 52 mesh to 10 cm; 27 cm by 35 cm.
Thread: D.M.C 6-strand embroidery floss:
Top
½ skein each of Pistachio Green (369), Emerald Green (913), Beaver Gray (647), Myrtle Gray (927), Almond Green (502); small amount each of Coffee Brown (938), Drab (610, 612, 613), Beige Brown (840), Umber (436), Copper Green (831), Beige (3047), Hazel-nut Brown (422), Pistachio Green (319, 367), Scarab Green (3347), Saffron (726)` and Canary Yellow (972).
Bottom
½ skein each of Yellow Green (733), Sage Green (3013), Dull

Mauve (315), Faded Pink (224), Seagull Gray (452); small amount each of Antique Gray (535), Coffee Brown (898), Drab (610, 612, 613), Smoke Gray (640), Beige Brown (840), Beige (3047), Red Brown (918, 919), Golden Yellow (782), Moss Green (937), Apricot Pink (945) and Yellow Green (730).
Frame: 34 cm by 41.5 cm (inside measurements).
Finished size: 21 cm by 28.5 cm (embroidered area).
Gauge: One square of design equals one square mesh of fabric.
Directions: Match centers of fabric and design and embroider. Mount and frame.

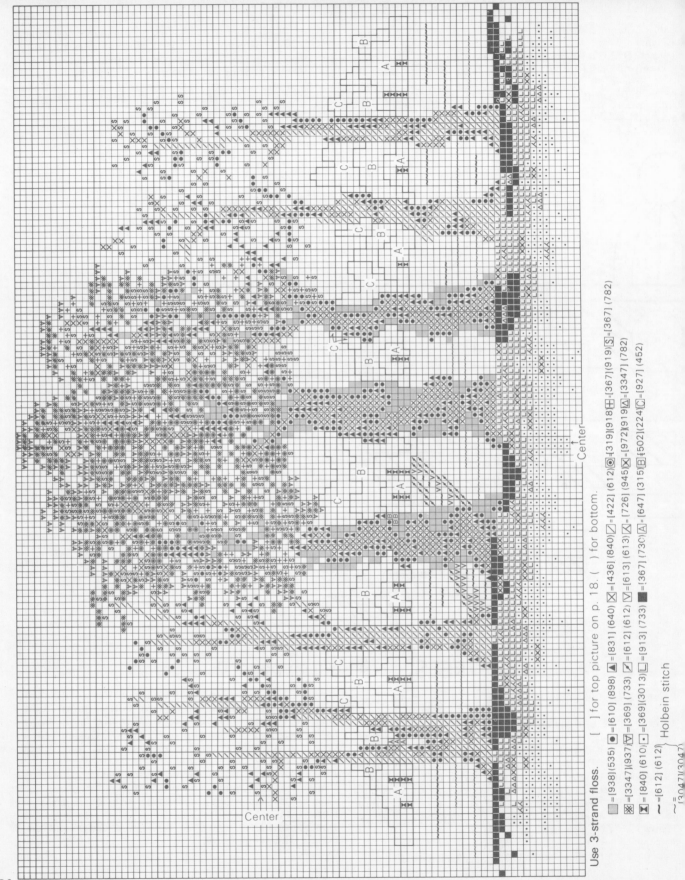

Use 3-strand floss.　　[ ] for top picture on p. 18. ( ) for bottom.

∨=[938]﹙535﹚　●=[610]﹙898﹚　▲=[831]﹙640﹚　⊠=[436]﹙840﹚　◪=[422]﹙612﹚　◉=[319]﹙918﹚　⊞=[367]﹙919﹚　⑤=[367]﹙782﹚

※=[3347]﹙937﹚　▽=[369]﹙733﹚　✓=[612]﹙612﹚　▼=[613]﹙613﹚　◩=[726]﹙945﹚　⊠=[972]﹙919﹚　△=[3347]﹙782﹚

☒=[840]﹙610﹚　⦁=[369]﹙3013﹚　▫=[913]﹙733﹚　◧=[367]﹙730﹚　▲=[647]﹙315﹚　🅱=[502]﹙224﹚　ⓒ=[927]﹙452﹚

∼=[612]﹙612﹚　⎫
　　　　　　　⎬ Holbein stitch
∼=[3047]﹙3047﹚⎭

86

GIRLS IN THE COUNTRY   Shown on page 29

Fabric: Cream Irish linen, 41 cm by 51 cm. Lining, 41 cm by 51 cm.

Thread: D.M.C 6-strand embroidery floss:
½ skeins each of Brilliant Green (701), Beaver Gray (647); 1 skein each of Moss Green (937), Parakeet Green (904), Laurel Green (988), Emerald Green (909), Beaver Gray (645); ½ skein each of Peacock Green (993), Flame Red (608); small amount each of Cerise (603, 604), Canary Yellow (972), Indian Red (3042), Parma Violet (209), Umber (739), Azure Blue (3325) and White.

Boder ribbon: 132 cm.

Finished size: 34.5 cm by 48 cm.

Directions: Transfer deign to fabric and embroider. Finish with border ribbon as shown in Finishing Diagram.

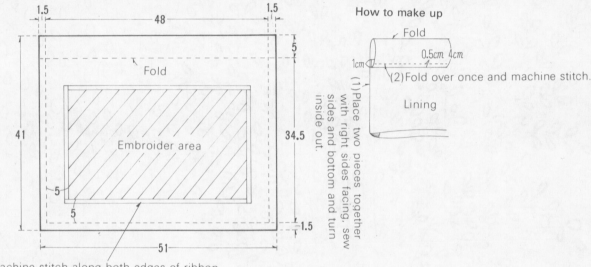

Machine stitch along both edges of ribbon.

How to make up

(1) Place two pieces together with right sides facing, sew sides and bottom and turn inside out.

(2) Fold over once and machine stitch.

Lining

Modified French knot

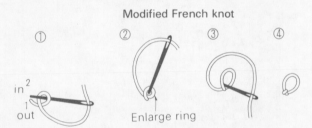

Enlarge ring

(Design on next page)

Lazy daisy (909)
Outline (647)

Lazy daisy (701)

Satin and (645
3-strand fl

Outline (209)

Outline filling

Outline filling (972)

French knot and △ (739) 3-strand floss

(701) Straight
Outline (701)
Straight (988)
French knot (604)

French knot (972)

Z Z
× ×
× (3325)
Z
(209)

Outline filling

French knot (645) Outline Satin

(739)(645)

Long & short and 3-strand floss

(645) Straight Outline

Outline Couched trellis

(993)

Actual Size

Use 4-strand floss unless otherwise indicated.

Outline Fly } (993)

Lazy daisy (904)

Outline (645)

Lazy daisy Back } (988)

Open buttonhole Outline Satin } (608)

(3325)

Coral (972)

French knot variation and (701) 6-strand floss

Outline (988)

(3042)

French knot variation and (937) 6-strand floss

Straight (993)

Outline

Darning } (988) Straight

Long & short (972)

Fill in with coral

(647) (645)

Long & short and 3-strand floss (603)

Lazy daisy (604) (701)

Outline filling (White)

Twisted chain (647)

Outline (701)

THE LITTLE MATCH GIRL Shown on page 27

Actual Size
*Use 3-strand floss unless otherwise indicated.

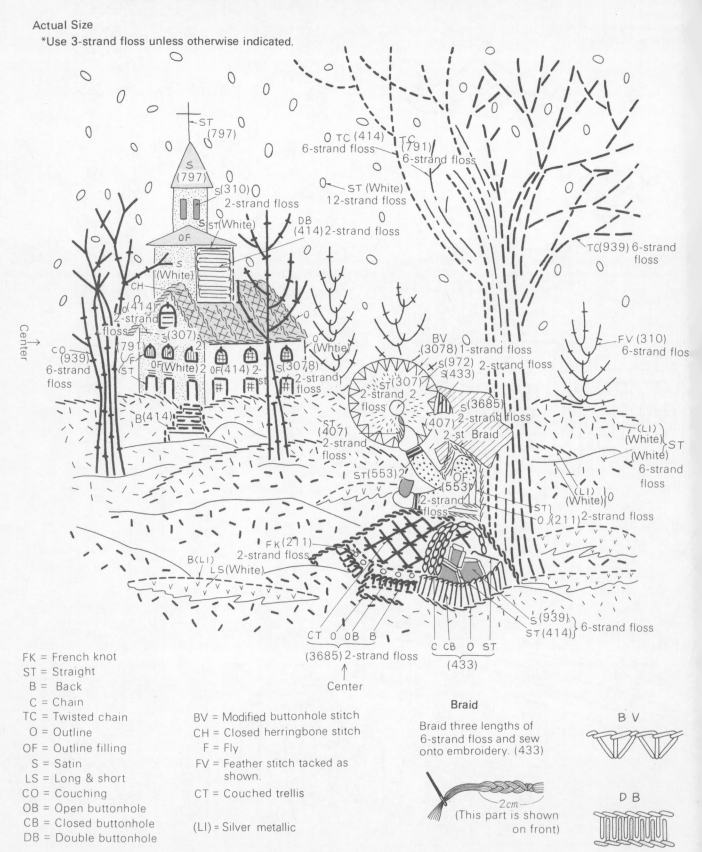

ST (797)

S (797)

s(310) O
2-strand floss

S ST (White)

DB (414) 2-strand floss

O TC (414) 6-strand floss

TC (791) 6-strand floss

ST (White) 12-strand floss

TC (939) 6-strand floss

S (White)

CH

o (414) 2-strand floss

CO (939) 6-strand floss

S (791) (F) (ST)

S (307)

OF (White)

OF (414) 2-strand floss

(White)

S (3078) 2-strand floss

BV (3078) 1-strand floss

s (972) 2-strand floss

S (433)

ST (307) 2-strand floss

S (3685) 2-strand floss

(407) 2-strand floss

2-st Braid

FV (310) 6-strand floss

B (414)

ST (407) 2-strand floss

ST (553) 2

OF (553) 2-strand floss

(LI) (White) ST (White) 6-strand floss

(LI) (White)

O (211) 2-strand floss

FK (211) 2-strand floss

B (LI)

LS (White)

S (939) ST (414) } 6-strand floss

CT O OB B (3685) 2-strand floss
↑ Center

C CB O ST (433)

Center →

FK = French knot
ST = Straight
 B = Back
 C = Chain
TC = Twisted chain
 O = Outline
OF = Outline filling
 S = Satin
LS = Long & short
CO = Couching
OB = Open buttonhole
CB = Closed buttonhole
DB = Double buttonhole

BV = Modified buttonhole stitch
CH = Closed herringbone stitch
 F = Fly
FV = Feather stitch tacked as shown.
CT = Couched trellis

(LI) = Silver metallic

Braid

Braid three lengths of 6-strand floss and sew onto embroidery. (433)

2cm
(This part is shown on front)

B V

D B

90

Fabric: Cobalt blue Irish linen, 21 cm square.
Thread: D.M.C 6-strand embroidery floss:
1 skein each of White, Indigo (939); ½ skein each of Cornflower Blue (791), Royal Blue (797), Ash Gray (414), Black (310), small amount each of Raspberry Red (3685), Plum (553), Parma Violet (211), Chestnut (407), Umber (433), Canary Yellow (972), Lemon Yellow (307) and Light Yellow (3078). Small amount of silver metallic.
Frame: White, 15 cm square (inside measurements).
Finished size: Same size as frame.
Directions: Match centers of fabric and design, and transfer design to fabric. Embroider. Mount and frame.

FRUIT STORE AT SUNSET   Shown on page 28

Fabric: Unbleached linen, 33 cm by 28 cm for each picture.
Thread: D.M.C 6-strand embroidery floss:
Left
1½ skeins each of Tangerine Yellow (741), Mahogany (300); 1 skein of Dark Brown (3033); small amount each of Royal Blue (996), Forget-me-not Blue (828), Brilliant Green (702, 703, 704), Emerald Green (911, 955), Lemon Yellow (307, 445), Buttercup Yellow (444), Tangerine Yellow (743), Geranium Red (892), Cerise (602, 604), Soft Pink (899), Umber (436, 738, 739), Fire Red (900), Plum (552), White and Black (310).
Right
1½ skeins each of Royal Blue (797), Cerise (602); 1 skein of Greenish Gray (598); small amount each of Royal Blue (796, 996), Greenish Gray (597), Brilliant Green (702, 703, 704), Emerald Green (911, 912, 955), Garnet Red (326), Geranium Red (892), Cerise (603), Soft Pink (818, 899), Peony Rose (957), Tangerine Yellow (741, 743), Buttercup Yellow (444), Lemon Yellow (307), Umber (436), Smoke Gray (822), Mahogany (300), Plum (552), Parma Violet (209), Ash Gray (318, 415), Flame Red (606), Poppy (666), Dark Brown (3033), White and Black (310).
Finished size: 23 cm by 18 cm (size of display panel).
Directions: Match centers of fabric and design, and transfer design to fabric. Embroider. Mount onto display panel.

(Design on next page)

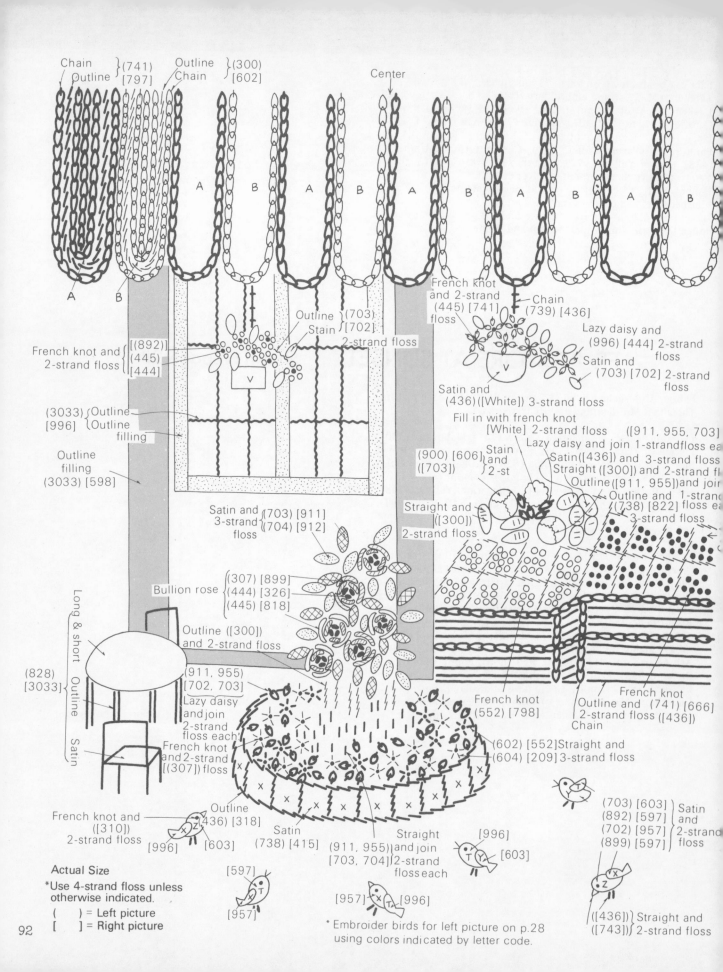

GEOMETRIC DESIGNS A & B   Shown on pages 36 & 37

Fabric: White Indian cloth, 52 mesh to 10 cm, 24 cm square.
Thread: D.M.C 6-strand embroidery floss:

A

1 skein of Royal Blue (995); ½ skein each of Royal Blue (820), Peacock Green (991); small amount each of Canary Yellow (973), Black (310), Fire Red (947), Greenish Gray (598), Flame Red (606) and Emerald Green (910).

B

1 skein of Flame Red (606); ½ skein each of Episcopal Purple (718), Plum (552); small amount each of Black (310), Emerald Green (910), Soft Pink (899), Canary Yellow (973) and Tangerine Yellow (740).

Frame: 34 cm square (inside measurements).
Finished size: 17.5 cm square (embroidered area).
Directions: Match centers of fabric and design, and cross-stitch. Mount and frame.

Use 3-strand floss.

( ) = Color key of A

[ ] = Color key of B

☒ = (995)[606]
◉ = (991)[522]
▨ = (820)[718]
■ = (310)[310]
A = (973)[606]
B = (947)[899]
C = (973)[910]
D = (598)[973]
E = (606)[899]
F = (973)[718]
G = (820)[740]
H = (910)[910]

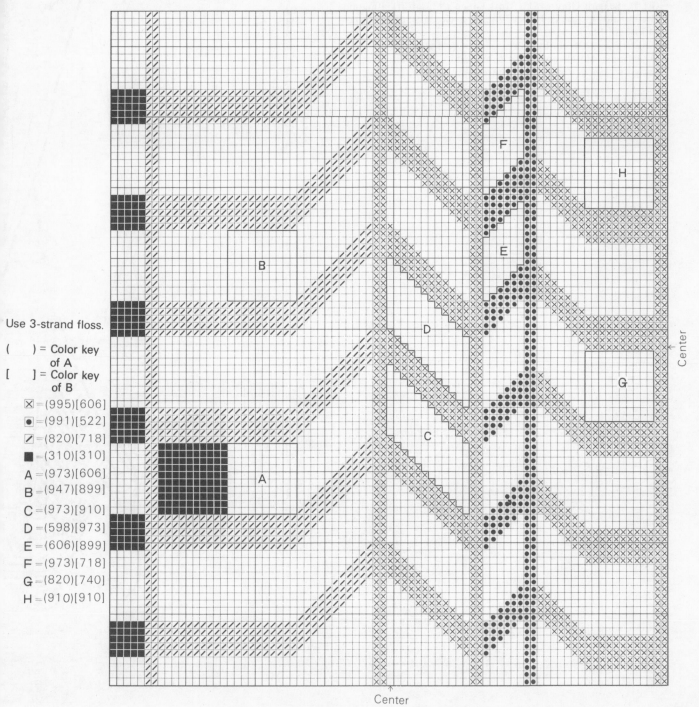

93

PASTORAL SCENE

Shown on page 20, left

Fabric: Unbleached, lightweight canvas, 36 cm by 28 cm.
Thread: D.M.C 6-strand embroidery floss:
1 skein of Drab (610); ½ skein each of Peacock Green (991),
Copper Green (830), Yellow Green (733), Fire Red (946),
Brilliant Green (700), Pistachio Green (320); small amount
each of Sevres Blue (799), Myrtle Gray (926), Ash Gray
(414), Seagull Gray (451), Moss Green (936, 470), Emerald
Green (909), Royal Blue (796), Ivy Green (500), Umber
(436) and Black (310).
Finished size: 26 cm by 18 cm (size of display panel).
Directions: Match centers of fabric and design, and transfer
design to fabric. Embroider. Mount onto panel.

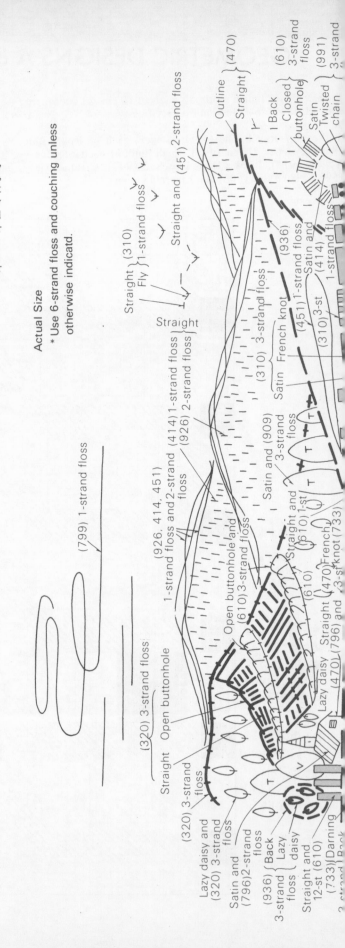

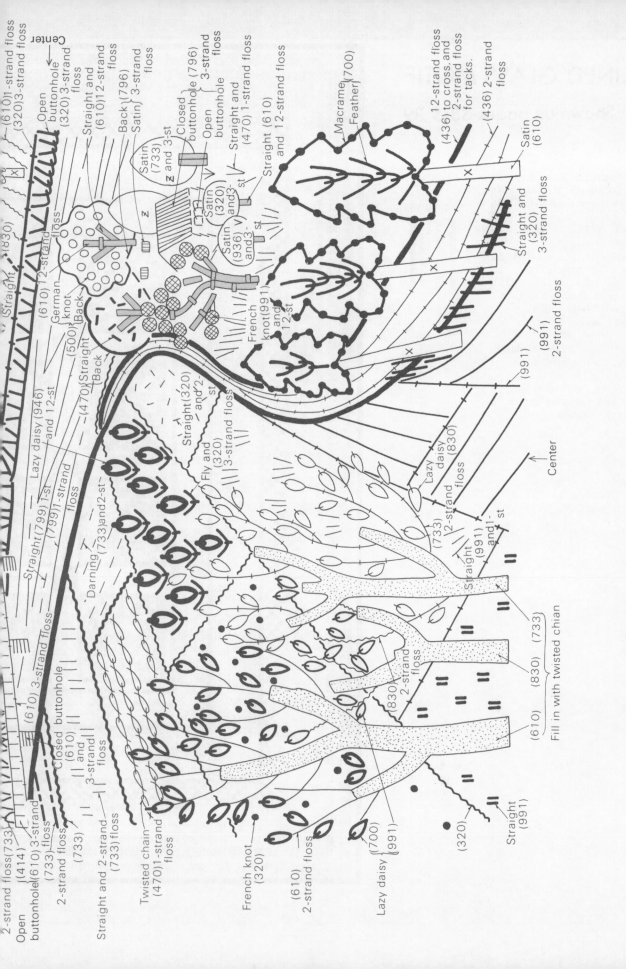

2-strand floss (733)(1-830)
Open } (414)
buttonhole(610) 3-strand
(733) floss
2-strand floss
(733)
Straight and 2-strand
(733) floss
Twisted chain
(470) 1-strand floss
Darning (733) and 2-st
(799) 1-strand
floss
Lazy daisy (946)
and 12-st
Straight (799) 1-st
(610) 12-strand
German-floss
(500) knot } Back
(470) Straight
(470) Straight } Back

(610) 1-strand floss
(320) 3-strand floss
Center
Open
buttonhole
(320) 3-strand
floss
Straight and
(610) 12-strand
floss
Back } (796)
Satin } 3-strand
floss
Satin
(733)
z and 3-st
Satin
(320)
and 3-st
Satin
(936)
and 3-st
Closed buttonhole (796)
Open 3-strand
buttonhole floss
Straight and
(470) 1-strand floss
Straight (610)
and 12-st
French knot (991)
and
12-st

Macrame (700)
Feather (700)

12-strand floss
(436) to cross, and
2-strand floss
for tacks.

(436) 2-strand
floss

Satin
(610)
Straight and
(320)
3-strand floss

(991)
2-strand floss

(991)

Lazy
daisy
(830)
2-strand
floss

Center

Straight
(733)
2-strand
floss

Straight (991)
and 1-
st

Straight (320)
and 2-
st
Fly and
(320)
3-strand floss

Closed buttonhole
(610)
3-strand } || and
floss (733)

French knot
(320)

(610)
2-strand floss

Lazy daisy (700)
(991)

(320)

Straight (991)

(610) (830) (733)

(830)
2-strand
floss

Fill in with twisted chian

STAINED GLASS MOTIF

Shown on pages 38 & 39

Fabric: Cream Java cloth, 26 mesh to 10 cm; 83 cm by 74 cm. White cotton, 65 cm by 56 cm.

Thread: D.M.C 6-strand embroidery floss:

15 skeins of Black (310); 12 skeins of Yellow Green (732); 9 skeins of Myrtle Gray (926); 8 skeins of Garnet Red (326); 2 skeins of Beige (3024).

Finished size: Refer to diagram.

Gauge: One square of design equals one square mesh of fabric.

Directions: Cross-stitch as indicated and finish as shown in Finishing Diagram.

Hanging strap

*Use 6-strand floss.

■ = 310
⊡ = 732
⊚ = 326
△ = 3024
⊠ = 926

Cen

96

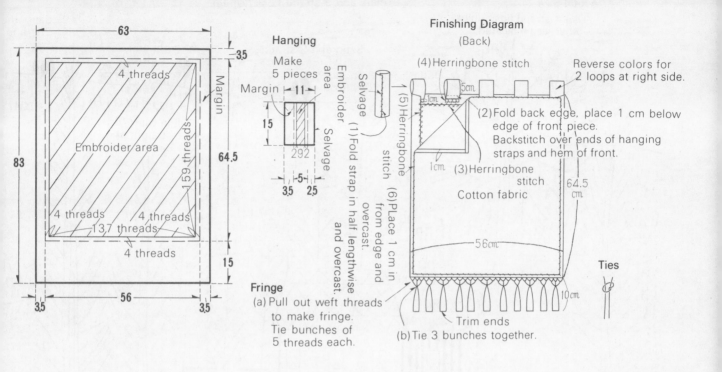

Hanging

Make 5 pieces

Margin

Embroider area

Selvage

Selvage

(1) Fold strap in half lengthwise and overcast.

Fringe
(a) Pull out weft threads to make fringe. Tie bunches of 5 threads each.

Finishing Diagram
(Back)

(4) Herringbone stitch

Reverse colors for 2 loops at right side.

(5) Herringbone stitch

(2) Fold back edge, place 1 cm below edge of front piece. Backstitch over ends of hanging straps and hem of front.

(6) Herringbone stitch

(3) Herringbone stitch

(6) Place 1 cm in from edge and overcast.

Cotton fabric

Ties

Trim ends

(b) Tie 3 bunches together.

HOUSE AND POND   Shown on page 20, right

Fabric: Blue Oxford cloth, 92 mesh to 10 cm; 36 cm by 28 cm.

Thread: D.M.C 6-strand embroidery floss:
½ skein each of Brilliant Green (701, 702, 703), Indigo (334), Antique Gray (535); Violet Mauve (327); small amount each of Soft Pink (3326), Magenta Rose (962), Peacock Green (991) and White.

Finished size: 26 cm by 18 cm (size of display panel).

Directions: Match centers of fabric and design, and transfer design to fabric. Embroider. Mount onto panel.

Threaded Running Stitch

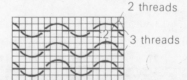

2 threads

3 threads

Embroider running stitch, then run another thread back and forth through running stitches.

(Design on next page)

Acutal Size
*Use 4-strand floss unless
otherwise indicated.

Outline and 3-strand floss (White)

Satin and 2-strand (535) floss

(3326) Satin and (White) 2-strand

Outline and 3-strand (704) floss

Straight and (535) 2-strand floss

Fill in with (704) straight and 3-strand floss

Outline and (702)3-strand floss

Fill in with straight(702)

Zig zag (962) Outline Back

Satin (962) 3-st

Outline and (327) 3-strand floss

Stain and (535) 3-strand floss

Chain filling and 3-strand floss(White)

Coral (3326)

Open buttonhole (962)

(327)(535)

Outline and 3-strand floss

Center

Fill in with threaded running (334)
Refer to diagram

Outline (3326)

Satin and 2-strand floss (White)

Straight and 1-strand floss (535)

Outline Straight Fly (991) 3-strand floss

Outline filling and (535) 2-strand floss

French knot (962)

Fill in with straight (701)

98

Center

SWEET AND COOL CHECKERBOARD

Shown on page 40

Fabric: Off-white Irish linen for blue motif and pink Irish linen for pink motif, 25 cm square each.
Thread: D.M.C 6-strand embroidery floss:
Tints of Blue
1 skein of Royal Blue (796); ½ skein of Sevres Blue (799); small amount each of Brilliant Green (702), Sevres Blue (798, 800), Royal Blue (996), Lemon Yellow (307) and White.

Tints of Pink
½ skein each of Soft Pink (818), Cerise (601); small amount each of Peony Rose (957), Soft Pink (776, 819), Brilliant Green (703), Umber (436, 738) and Hazel-nut Brown (422).
Finished size: 15 cm square (size of display panel).
Directions: Match centers of fabric and design and embroider. Mount onto panel.

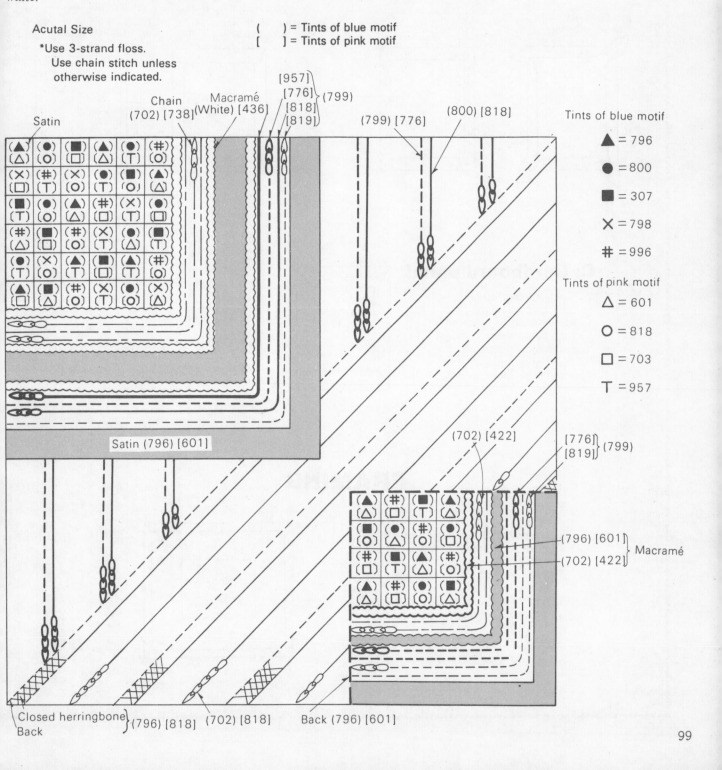

Acutal Size

*Use 3-strand floss.
 Use chain stitch unless
 otherwise indicated.

(   ) = Tints of blue motif
[   ] = Tints of pink motif

Satin

Chain (702) [738]
Macramé (White) [436]

[957]
[776]
[818] (799)
[819]

(799) [776]

(800) [818]

Tints of blue motif

▲ = 796
● = 800
■ = 307
✕ = 798
= 996

Tints of pink motif

△ = 601
O = 818
□ = 703
T = 957

Satin (796) [601]

(702) [422]

[776]
[819] (799)

(796) [601]
(702) [422]

Macramé

Closed herringbone
Back

(796) [818]   (702) [818]   Back (796) [601]

MOUNTING & FRAMING

A: Wooden canvas frame

Wooden frames of a variety of sizes are available at frame shops.

(1) Place frame on wrong side of embroidered fabric, matching corners, and staple fabric to frame starting at center of sides and working toward corners.

(2) Pull fabric at corners to stretch tightly over frame and miter.

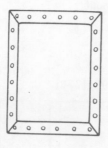

B: Adhesive styrofoam panel

Available in frame shops.

(1) Place non-adhesive side of panel on wrong side of embroidered fabric. Fold fabric over onto back of panel and fix in place.
If fabric is heavy, cut excess fabric at corners. Glue corners.

(2) Place a piece of cloth or paper, slightly smaller than the panel, onto adhesive back and fix in place. Use two-sided tape or glue to attach backing where it overla onto fabric

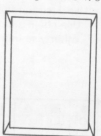

C: Cardboard panel

Cut cardboard to finished size, place on wrong side of fabric and fold fabric onto back of cardboard. Fix fabric in place with glue or two-sided tape. Miter corners.

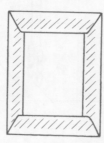

FRAMING

Large frames such as those shown on pages 11 and 35 may be used to enhance the embroidery. Frames and pasteboard mountings are available at frame shops.
(Finished size indicated in the instructions is for the embroidered area only.)

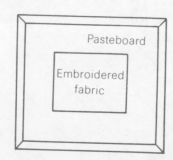